The True Meaning of Wealth

Money is not wealth and having money is not always an appropriate measurement of wealth. In fact, taken by itself, money has no value; what use is a bundle of paper or coins with pictures of deceased people on them? It is only the things that money can buy that gives money value. After all, how useful would a million dollars be if you were shipwrecked on a desert island? How wealthy is a successful business-man who earns a six-figure salary but whose work-load prevents him from spending time with his children? And who is wealthier, a millionaire who has terminal cancer, or a man with an empty bank account who enjoys perfect health? Real wealth can be judged only in the quality of life you lead. Only a person who is able to live his own life in his own way is truly wealthy.

BY ADAM J. JACKSON

The Ten Secrets of Abundant Happiness
The Ten Secrets of Abundant Wealth
The Ten Secrets of Abundant Love
The Ten Secrets of Abundant Health

Published by HarperPaperbacks

The
TEN SECRETS
of
ABUNDANT WEALTH

*A Modern Parable of Wisdom
and Happiness That Will
Change Your Life*

ADAM J. JACKSON

HarperPaperbacks
A Division of HarperCollinsPublishers

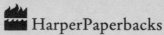 **HarperPaperbacks**
A Division of HarperCollins*Publishers*
10 East 53rd Street, New York, N.Y. 10022-5299

This is a work of fiction. The characters, incidents, and
dialogues are products of the author's imagination and are not to
be construed as real. Any resemblance to actual events or
persons, living or dead, is entirely coincidental.

A trade paperback edition of this book was published in 1996
in Great Britain by Thorsons, an imprint of
HarperCollins*Publishers*.

ISBN 0-06-104423-7

HarperCollins®, 🔥®, and HarperPaperbacks™
are trademarks of HarperCollins*Publishers* Inc.

Cover and interior illustrations by Joan Perrin Falquet

First HarperPaperbacks printing: October 1996

Printed in the United States of America

Visit HarperPaperbacks on the World Wide Web at
http://www.harpercollins.com/paperbacks

❖ 10 9 8 7 6 5 4 3 2 1

*This book is dedicated with love
to the memory of Annie Woolf.*

Contents

Acknowledgments

I would like to thank all those people who have helped me in my work and in the writing of this book. I am particularly grateful to:

My literary agent, Sara Menguc, and her assistant, Georgia Glover, for all their efforts and work on my behalf.

Everyone at Thorsons, but especially Erica Smith for her enthusiasm and constructive comments throughout the writing of the book, and Fiona Brown who edited the manuscript.

My mother, who always encouraged me to write, and remains a constant source of inspiration and love to me; my father for his encouragement, guidance and help in all my work, and all of my family and friends for their love.

And finally, to Karen—my wife, my best friend, and my most candid editor. Words cannot express my love for the one person who has always had faith in me and believed in my work.

Whatever the mind of a man can concieve
and believe . . . it can achieve.

W. Clement Stone

Introduction

> When riches begin to come, they come so quickly,
> in such great abundance, that one wonders where
> they have been hiding during all those lean years.
>
> NAPOLEON HILL
> *THINK AND GROW RICH*

By the time we reach the age of 65, over ninety percent of us are either dead, or dead broke! Only eight percent of men and two percent of women are financially independent, and less than one percent of the population are wealthy. But why? What do those one percent know that the others don't? Are they more intelligent? Better educated? Do they work harder? Are they simply lucky, blessed by fate?

These questions bothered me for many years. If wealth is something to which we all aspire, why do less than one in every hundred of us achieve it? Why do so many struggle to make ends meet, feeling trapped, even powerless to fulfill their dreams? And then one day, I met an extraordinary old man who told me about the secrets of Abundant Wealth—ten principles through which anyone can create not just wealth in their lives, but wealth in abundance!

Abundant Wealth is not just a matter of the size of your bank account or number or value of the possessions you own; it is rather having sufficient means to be able to live your own life, in your own way. I discovered that we all have the power to be wealthy. It doesn't matter what our circumstances are; whether we are young or old, married or single, black or white. External circumstances—the state of the economy, the weather, government policy—do not control our lives; we do! And it is when we begin to take control, to take responsibility for our lives, that we realize the power that we have to make changes and to fulfill our dreams.

Unlike many other parables, the characters in this book are based upon composites of real people although I have, of course, changed their names. It is my hope that their stories will inspire you to follow their example and create Abundant Wealth in your own life.

Adam Jackson
Hertfordshire
November 1995

The
WALK
in the
PARK

It was cold and dark when the young man walked out of the front door and stepped onto the street, but no colder or darker than could be expected for 6 A.M. on the first Monday in February. The street lamps were still lit and there was already a small, but steady, stream of traffic on the roads. Not long ago, he would have struggled to get out of bed by 8 A.M., but for the last few months he had felt restless, his sleep patterns had become disturbed and sporadic.

He walked across the road and made his way up the hill toward the park. It was a routine his father had always followed, a brisk walk through the park at dawn to open the lungs and clear the head before the day ahead. Walk through the park at sunrise, his father had always advised, and you will find that new ideas, inspiration and solutions to your most pressing problems often come to you.

"It's as if the angels are whispering to you," his father would say. But, in the two weeks that he had been taking these early morning walks, he had heard no whispers, he had had no ideas, no inspiration, and there were no solutions to his problems.

1

As he walked past the large detached houses he imagined how wonderful it would be to be wealthy enough to afford to live in such a grand residence. Wouldn't it be fantastic, he thought, if he were able to buy and live in such a house. His mind wandered, and for the briefest of moments, images of living in one of these houses flickered in his head. Relaxing in the bright, spacious living rooms, having spare double bedrooms for family and friends to stay, and to just sit and enjoy a beautiful garden on a sunny day would be his idea of heaven.

But the daydream ended and his thoughts returned to reality as he passed the last house before the park. The reality was that he had never been wealthy enough to afford even a small terraced cottage let alone such a huge, detached property and, short of winning the national lottery, he would probably never have the means necessary to purchase one of those houses. Financially, life was, and always had been, and probably always would be, a struggle.

Once inside the park, the young man headed for the running track, and increased his stride to a brisk pace. As he walked, he couldn't help feeling that fate had conspired against him. If only he had been born into a wealthy family. If only he had had the luck and opportunities that seem to come other people's way.

But the truth was that the young man's problems were no different from the majority of the population. At the end of each month he was usually overdrawn, wherever he turned there was a bill waiting for him. Somehow—goodness only knows how—he had always managed to get by, but that was all. And, in the past few months, with the economy depressed, just getting by was becoming more and more of a struggle. He seemed to be working longer hours for slightly less pay, and now he couldn't see himself ever getting ahead, let alone being able to afford the things he used to dream about.

He had once dreamed of becoming a famous writer, of supporting a family and owning his own house, but there was no way, given his present circumstances, that his dreams could be realized, and deep down he couldn't see it ever happening. When he was younger he might have had the courage to leave his job and search for something he would be happier doing, but saddled with mounting bills, he couldn't afford to lose his job.

He was trapped; trapped in a job which not only did not pay particularly well, but for which he had little interest and no enthusiasm. Many of his colleagues in the office also seemed bored and disinterested in their work. To them, as to him, the job was simply a means of making a living, of surviving.

And so, over the years, the young man had given up on his boyhood hopes and dreams. All he dared hope for now was to get by . . . as best he could. As he walked through the park all he could do was hope and pray that if angels did exist, one of them would whisper to him— some idea, some piece of inspiration that would some-how change his fate.

But so engrossed was the young man in his thoughts that he hadn't noticed the sun rising above the oak trees to the east of the park, or the song of the robins over-head, and he was completely unaware of the old man who was walking by his side.

The MEETING

A voice startled the young man from his thoughts. "Good morning." He turned to find an elderly Chinese man by his side.

"Good morning," he replied, glancing briefly at the old man. He was short, his head barely level with the young man's shoulders, dressed in a black track suit.

"Mind if I join you?" asked the old man.

"Be my guest. If you can keep up," answered the young man.

The old man smiled. "I'll do my best," he said, increasing his pace. "You look like a man with a load on his mind."

"Not really," said the young man without looking up.

"You know, in my country we believe that every problem brings with it a gift; every adversity contains within it the seed of an equivalent or greater benefit."

"Hmmf!" sniffed the young man dismissively.

"It applies to everything ... even money problems," said the old man.

The young man caught his breath on the old man's words and turned to face him. "What possible benefit can there be in having money problems?" he asked.

4

The Meeting

"Money problems open the path to abundant wealth—riches beyond your dreams," answered the old man.

"How is that possible?" demanded the young man.

"Did you know that many of the world's richest and greatest men were at one time penniless or bankrupt?" said the old man.

"No," said the young man, shaking his head.

"Abraham Lincoln was declared bankrupt at the age of 35, yet he went on to become one of the most powerful men in the history of the United States of America. Og Mandino was a drunk vagrant, but he went on to become a best-selling writer, and Walt Disney was bankrupt on several occasions before he went on to create the Disney empire."

The young man was astonished. He had always thought that being penniless or bankrupt was a fate that only happened to life's failures and losers.

"But how is that possible?" he asked. "How can someone profit from being penniless?'

"It's quite simple." The old man smiled. "People don't search for abundance in their lives when they are comfortable. They need inspiration or desperation to begin to change their lives. A few people find inspiration but many, many more change because they are forced to change.

"You see, when you are desperate you begin to ask yourself questions and the nature of those questions shapes your destiny."

The color was slowly returning to the young man's face but his expression was still one of disbelief.

"Let me ask you this," continued the old man. "What were you thinking when I interrupted you?'

"I'm not sure. I suppose I was wondering why certain things had happened to me."

"And where do you think that question will lead?"

"I don't know," admitted the young man.

"Exactly!" exclaimed the old man. "It leads to 'don't know.' Or worse it leads to false answers. 'Why' questions always do. Your brain will always search for an answer to any question you ask; 'Why' questions produce no hope, no solutions and no future. 'Why did it happen to me?', 'Why am I in this mess?', 'Why can't I get ahead?'—these questions lead nowhere. Great men ask different questions, they ask 'How' and 'What' questions—'How can I improve the quality of my life?' or even better, 'What do I need to do to create wealth in my life?'"

"I don't know," said the young man. "It's answers I need, not questions."

"But if you want to find the right answer," said the old man, "you first have to ask the right question. It is written in the Bible: 'Seek and you shall find, ask and it shall be given to you.'"

"That sounds nice, but life isn't that simple."

"How do you know? Have you ever tried?" said the old man. "Perhaps life is simpler than you think."

"Well it doesn't seem so simple to me," said the young man. "Whatever I do, I can't seem to get ahead. I've tried everything, but nothing seems to work."

"Don't forget the golden rule of problem solving," said the old man.

"Which is?"

"When you think you have exhausted all the possibilities, remember one thing . . . you haven't!"

"That's all very well, but I don't know what else to do," replied the young man. "I have never been wealthy and I probably never will be. Perhaps I just don't have what it takes."

"And what does it take exactly that you don't have?" said the old man.

"I don't know. For a start, you need money to make money."

"What makes you think that? Did you know that Aristotle Onassis started his career with less than $200 dollars with no university degree and no rich relatives, yet he became one of the richest men who ever lived?"

The young man shrugged his shoulders. "Maybe he was just lucky," he said.

"Most wealthy people started out with little or no capital. Anita Roddick created her cosmetics company by making up toiletries in a garage. Bill Gates, one of the richest men in the world, built his fortune from innovations in the computer industry. Anthony Robbins, the best-selling author and one of the foremost leaders in personal development was, at one time, financially broke and living in a small studio apartment, yet he managed to turn his life around within the space of a year, becoming a millionaire and purchasing a 10,000-foot castle overlooking the ocean. Do you really think that their successes were the result of luck?"

"Well, maybe not entirely," replied the young man. "But you have to get a lucky break sometime, don't you?"

"There is one very important trait you will find in every person who has accumulated wealth—personal responsibility! They all take responsibility for their actions and decisions. They don't blame the economy or the government or the weather or their childhood for their problems. Wealthy people don't wait for lucky breaks or the right circumstances, they go out and create them. They don't look for excuses, they look for solutions. They are committed to succeeding."

"You may be right," said the young man. "All I know is that I have always struggled financially. Perhaps it's my fate."

"The only fate you have is what you make," said the old man. "Just because you never have been wealthy, doesn't mean that you never will be. The most important lesson you can ever learn in life is that your future does not have to be the same as your past. It is only when you do the things that you have always done, that you get the things you have always got."

The two men walked past the lake to the north side of the park. Two joggers brushed past them, their breath forming a fine mist in the cold air. The young man thought carefully about what the old man said. There was no doubt that there was some sense in what he was saying, but he was still not convinced.

"You don't need to have money to make money," explained the old man. "You don't need to have rich relatives or a university degree or a lucky break. All you need to create wealth in your life, you already have."

"You think it's that simple?" said the young man.

"Of course. There is no luck involved. You have the power to create your destiny just as much as anyone else."

"But surely, you're not suggesting that *anybody* can become wealthy?" demanded the young man.

"Of course I am. And do you know, most people in the world are already wealthy, but they don't even know it!"

"What do you mean?" said the young man. "People with any real wealth would know about it."

"You'd think so, wouldn't you?" said the old man. "But they don't. You are a typical example. You think you are poor because you struggle to pay your bills?"

"Yes, but how did you . . . ?" said the young man.

"You have continuous running water, clean water—something that until a few centuries ago, was a scarcity and in some parts of the world today, still is. You have access to information—the most valuable resource there is—through public libraries; information on virtually any subject you care to mention, much of which is denied to people in other parts of the world. You have enough food, sufficient clothing, shelter. You have a telephone enabling you to contact someone instantly even if they are on the other side of the world; you have a television, bringing news and entertainment into your home every day. You can purchase a range of foods that would have been unheard of fifty years ago.

"There are cars, trains and airplanes—all modes of transport out of the reach of the richest men up until the last century. So, you see, compared with all of the thousands of millions of people who have lived throughout history, you are very wealthy, wealthier than they would have ever dreamed possible.

"Money is not wealth," continued the old man, "and having money is not always an appropriate measurement of wealth. In fact, by itself, money has no value; what use is a bundle of paper or coins with pictures of deceased people on them? It is only the things that money can buy that gives money value. After all, how useful would a million dollars be if you were shipwrecked on a desert island? How wealthy is a successful businessman who earns a six-figure salary but whose workload prevents him from spending time with his children? And who is wealthier, a millionaire who has terminal cancer, or a man with an empty bank account but who enjoys perfect health?

"Real wealth can be judged only in the quality of the life you lead. Only a person who is able to live his own life in his own way is truly wealthy," said the old man.

The path the two men had taken led them through a large wooded area. The branches on the trees were beginning to bud early, the colors revealing that blossom was not far off. There was a brief moment's silence before the young man spoke.

"But money can improve the quality of your life," he said.

"Used wisely, yes, it can," acknowledged the old man. "But many people think that money will solve all their problems."

"Well, it would go a long way to solving my problems." The young man smiled.

"You may think so, but I can assure you it wouldn't," answered the old man emphatically.

The remark irritated the young man. What did this old man know about his problems anyway? But before he could argue his case, the old man continued. "What would you do if you won a million dollars?"

"I'd pay off my debts."

"Then what?"

"I'm not sure. First I'd celebrate and throw a party for my family and friends. Then I'd buy a new house with a swimming pool and a tennis court, a new car, a new TV, new furniture. Then I'd take my family on a holiday and I'd also give some money to some of my friends who need it."

"Then what?" said the old man.

"I don't know," confessed the young man. "I haven't thought about it before."

"What you have just said is similar to many, many people; people who dream of someday being wealthy. But in your answer lies the reason why they can never attain abundant wealth."

"What do you mean?" interjected the young man. "Some people win the lottery, some people become millionaires overnight."

"That is true, but their wealth is often temporary. Most of them end up as penniless as when they first bought their lottery ticket!"

The young man shook his head in disbelief.

"It's true," the old man assured him. "And the reason why they end up penniless? Because they never learned how to create or manage wealth. Consequently, they rarely accumulate wealth and, on the odd occasion when they do, they quickly lose it. They are like people who have been given a precious plant but have no idea how to nurture the plant; the soil it requires, the climate it needs to grow, the amount and frequency of the water it needs or the pests from which it must be protected. They may enjoy the fruits of the plant for a short time, but it will soon wither and die.

"Yet the man who studies the nature of the plant, understands the needs of the plant. He knows how to produce such a plant from a seedling. He knows how to look after the plant and so he is able to grow as many as he wishes.

"Wealth is a very precious thing, like the plant. We all have the power to create it, and to create it in abundance, but we must learn the secrets of creating and maintaining it.

"All money leads to nothing if we do not know how to handle it. Do you remember the story of the prodigal son?"

It sounded familiar but the young man could not recall the details.

"A rich landowner had two sons, the younger of which had no interest in learning about his father's business. Instead, he demanded his inheritance from his father so that he could venture into the world. Whilst saddened by his son's attitude, the father gave his son his inheritance and watched him depart. The son enjoyed parties and the fine things he bought with his money but it was not long before all his money had been spent. With no more than the clothes on his back, he returned ashamed and penniless to his father.

"The prodigal son began his journey with plenty of riches, but he quickly lost them all because he hadn't learned how to create income."

The two men reached the end of the wooded park land and began to follow the path ahead which led up a steep incline to the top of the hill.

"You see, wealth is not just about the amount of capital a man has," said the old man. "Capital can quickly be diminished. To be wealthy you need simply to have sufficient means to enable you to live according to your desired lifestyle."

"And how do you do that?" asked the young man.

The old man smiled. "You must first understand that this world and everything within it is governed by laws," he explained. "Natural laws. Many are well known; for instance, we know in physics of the law of gravity; drop an apple and it will fall to the ground. We know that, without oxygen, all life on this planet would not survive. But there are many laws—some relating to acquiring abundant wealth—which are not well known, and to most people remain secrets."

They were less than halfway up the hill and already the young man was struggling to catch his breath, but the old man beside him continued effortlessly. When they reached the top of the hill, the young man turned to the old man.

"So," he said, regaining his breath, "what are the secrets?"

"The secrets of Abundant Wealth, like all of Nature's secrets, are available to everyone. All you need do is ask the right questions of the right people. Here, this will help you," said the old man as he handed the young man a piece of paper. The young man hurriedly unfolded the paper but, to his surprise, he found no secrets, no wise words and no magic formulae—just a list of ten names and ten telephone numbers. But when he looked up, the old man had vanished.

He spun around, surveying the area, but apart from two people who were walking their dogs, there was no one to be seen.

"Excuse me," said the young man walking toward the two people who were walking their dogs. "Did you see where the old man who was walking with me went?"

The man and woman, both elderly, looked at each other before answering. "I didn't see anyone walking with you," said the man. "Did you, Ethel?" he asked his companion. The woman by his side shook her head.

"No," she said.

"But surely, you must have seen him; an elderly Chinese man in a black tracksuit," persisted the young man.

"I'm sorry," repeated the man. "I didn't see anybody with you."

The young man walked slowly back through the park retracing the steps he had taken. He couldn't understand it. How could the old man have vanished so quickly? And why hadn't the couple walking their dogs seen him? Perhaps he had imagined it all, daydreaming as he walked. But, as he put his hands into his pockets he realized that it couldn't have been a dream, the old man had been with him. There was evidence that he existed, a piece of paper containing ten names and ten telephone numbers.

The POWER of SUBCONSCIOUS BELIEFS

The young man telephoned all of the people on the old man's list as soon as he arrived home. He hesitated during the first few calls, unsure of how they would react to a total stranger claiming he had been given their name and telephone number by a mysterious old Chinese man. But he needn't have worried because they all knew of the old Chinese man and the secrets of Abundant Wealth. What is more, they all seemed to be genuinely delighted that he had called them. He arranged to meet each of them in turn over the following weeks.

The first person on the young man's list was a man by the name of Richard Appleby. Despite having a full schedule, Mr. Appleby willingly agreed to set aside time the following afternoon at 5 P.M. to meet the young man.

Mr. Appleby lived in a penthouse suite in one of the most exclusive areas of the city. When the young man entered the living room, he was immediately impressed by the magnificent view of the city at sunset. The entire south-facing wall was made up of four panelled windows offering panoramic views across the city. The setting sun draped the city's skyline in a cloak of amber and the scene glittered with lights from the office blocks and the flow of traffic and streetlights below.

"That's a fantastic view," admired the young man. "I've never seen the city look so spectacular."

"It is, isn't it." Mr. Appleby smiled. "The view is what sold the apartment to me. It doesn't matter what time of the day it is, I can just sit and watch it for hours."

The young man judged Mr. Appleby to be in his late forties. He was a small, athletic man with fair hair and bright blue eyes. Smartly but casually dressed, he wore a pair of cotton, beige trousers and a white open-collared shirt.

"So, you're interested in the secrets of Abundant Wealth?" he said as the young man sat down.

"Do you think that they really exist?" asked the young man.

"Of course," answered Mr. Appleby.

"What exactly are these secrets?" asked the young man.

"They are simply ten timeless principles which, when used, will enable virtually anybody to create not just wealth, but wealth in abundance."

"Anybody? Are you sure about that?" said the young man.

"Absolutely," said Mr. Appleby.

"But if everybody has the capability to be wealthy, why are so many of us struggling to make a living?"

"It is not what people are capable of that is important," said Mr. Appleby. "It's what they *believe* they are capable of. The average human mind and body is capable of great things, the main problem is that we don't believe that we are capable of them."

"I remember a long time ago going to a stage show in which a hypnotist selected members of the audience to be hypnotized. The hypnotist asked a man from the audience to lie down on a table; he then hypnotized the man and told him that his body was now as rigid as a piece of steel. Placing two chairs at either end of the table to support the man's head and feet, the hypnotist removed the table and the man's body remained supported just by two chairs, one under his head and the other under his feet. His body was rigid as steel because he believed that it was.

"Later in the same show, other people were hypnotized, but this time they were told by the hypnotist that they would not be able to lift the fountain pen which was lying on the table. That fountain pen, the hypnotist told them, was heavier than a two-ton truck. It could not be moved. 'Try anyway,' he suggested, 'but that pen is immovable.'

"One after the other they tried to lift that pen. I remember one man, in particular—a great, big strapping man who looked like a body builder. When he tried to lift the fountain pen, his face grimaced, sweat broke out on his forehead, and the muscles on his arm contracted so tightly that the veins were bulging . . . but he couldn't lift that pen! And the reason was not because he wasn't capable of lifting it—even a tiny baby has the strength to lift a pen—but he didn't *believe* that he could lift it. In fact, he was convinced that he couldn't.

"So you see, it's not necessarily what you're capable of achieving in life that is important, as what you believe that you're capable of achieving.

"This is the first secret of Abundant Wealth . . . the power of our subconscious beliefs."

"Our subconscious beliefs?" repeated the young man. "I don't understand how what we believe affects our wealth."

"Well, if a healthy, athletic man can't lift up a fountain pen just because he believes that it is impossible, what chance do you think a person has of becoming rich if he or she believes that it is virtually impossible?

"Fifteen years ago I was doing quite well. Nothing extraordinary, but I was comfortable and then one day I was laid off and suddenly I had no income, a mortgage to pay and all kinds of living expenses. I literally didn't know what I was going to do, and one night, being unable to sleep, I went for a walk along the river and it was then that I met someone who changed my life . . . an old Chinese man!"

"What happened?" said the young man, eager to find out more about the old man.

"He said something that stayed with me: 'Every adversity contains within it the seed of an equivalent or greater benefit.'"

"He said the same thing to me," said the young man.

"I couldn't understand it at the time," confided Mr. Appleby. "After all, how could losing my job and my sole source of income which had left me in desperate circumstances, contain any benefits? But looking back I can see that it was the best thing that could have happened to me because out of my desperation I was forced to create changes in my life, changes which I would not otherwise have made.

"I had always wanted to run my own business and be my own boss, and being laid off gave me an opportunity to do it. After learning the secrets of Abundant Wealth, I started up a management consultancy business from home and within my first year I made more than double the income that I had earned in my previous job."

"You're kidding," said the young man. "And you put your success down to the secrets of Abundant Wealth?"

"Definitely," confirmed Mr. Appleby. "William James, the American psychologist and philosopher who lived in the nineteenth century, said that the greatest discovery of his generation was that human beings could alter their lives, simply by altering their state of mind. And it is very true. Whatever you want in life, whether it is to be healthy or happy, or whether you want a loving relationship, or to be a millionaire, the first thing you need to do is to examine your attitudes and beliefs about what is possible and what isn't, because if you don't believe something is possible, it is very unlikely that you will ever get it."

The young man took out his notepad and pen. "Do you mind if I make some notes?" he asked.

"Not at all. It's a good idea." Mr. Appleby smiled. "Did you know," he continued, "that in medicine if one hundred people who are all suffering from the same disease are given a sugar tablet and told it is a miracle drug that will cure their disease, about forty percent of them will be cured simply because they believed the tablet would cure them? Similarly, as soon as most patients are told that they have an incurable disease, their condition rapidly deteriorates because they believe they are incurable.

"And what do you think your chances would be of attracting a loving relationship if you believed that you were unattractive? You would probably feel awkward mixing with people, and would sit at the back of the room at parties to try and make yourself as inconspicuous as possible. And even if you met someone to whom you were attracted, you would probably feel that you were not good enough for them.

"You see, in all areas of life, what matters most is our subconscious beliefs. And nowhere is it more important than in matters of money and wealth. In fact, the amount of money that you earn is usually exactly what you believe you are worth."

"Hold on a minute," said the young man. "I don't . . . "

"Are you happy with your present salary?" said Mr. Appleby.

"Not really, no," said the young man.

"Then why don't you ask for a raise?"

"Because I don't think I would get it."

"Well, you are less likely to get a raise if you don't ask," said Mr. Appleby smiling.

"That's true," said the young man. "But why would they increase my salary?"

"If you are worth more to them than your present salary, they'll pay you more. Obviously, you don't believe that you're worth more than your present level of pay. I interviewed a man last week for a job and would have been prepared to pay him a starting salary of $60,000. He was well qualified and perfect for the position. But when I asked him how much he wanted he said $30,000."

The young man wrote down some notes as Mr. Appleby continued. "Your circumstances are a mirror of your beliefs. If you don't believe that you can ever be wealthy, the chances are, you never will be. In fact, the biggest difference between a wealthy man and a poor man is not, as is commonly thought, the size of their bank accounts or the property that they own."

"What is it then?" asked the young man.

"Their beliefs! All wealthy people share specific beliefs about themselves and about money."

"You mean that wealthy people believe that they are capable of creating wealth?"

"Yes," answered Mr. Appleby. "But it goes a lot deeper than that. Let me explain it this way," said Mr. Appleby. "Obviously, in your conscious mind you want to accumulate wealth or you wouldn't be here discussing it."

The young man smiled. "Correct."

"So tell me, why do you want to be wealthy? What do you think having Abundant Wealth will add to your life?"

The young man thought for a moment. "Having wealth would bring freedom—freedom to go where I please, to do what I please, buy what I please; it would give me power, security, independence—I could start my own business."

"Good," said Mr. Appleby. "So, consciously you believe that money will give you greater freedom, power, security and independence?"

"Of course," answered the young man. "But surely most people would have given the same kind of answers. We all believe that money will change our lives," insisted the young man.

"Hold on, we haven't finished the exercise yet," said Mr. Appleby. "What I'd like you to do now is to think of all the things that you learned or heard about money and wealth while you were growing up."

"I don't know what you're getting at," said the young man.

"Well, what did your parents used to say about money?"

"Oh, I see. I remember my father always said that money didn't grow on trees."

"Okay. That's good. Anything else?"

"My mother used to say that money isn't everything and warned us that it doesn't bring happiness or buy love."

"Excellent. Anything else? What about religious beliefs about money?"

"What do you mean? That money is the root of all evil?" said the young man.

"Well, yes, that's one saying that we often hear, although I think you'll find that it is the *love* of money and not money itself which is considered to be the root of all evil."

Then it suddenly hit the young man. All of the things

he had learned about money whilst he was growing up were negative! He had been taught to believe that money was scarce, it wasn't important in life, it couldn't bring happiness or buy love: and it was the root of all evil which would prevent a person's soul entering the gates of heaven.

"Can you see how these subconscious beliefs conflict with your conscious beliefs? On the one hand you think money will bring you freedom, security, power and independence, but on the other hand, deep down you believe that if you accumulate any wealth you will be unhappy, unloved, sinful and barred from entering heaven. Your subconscious beliefs are therefore preventing you from being wealthy."

"I have never thought about it like that before," said the young man.

"There are other commonly held beliefs as well," continued Mr. Appleby. "Some people don't believe that they are worthy of having large amounts of money. Others believe that it is wrong or immoral to be wealthy. Why should I have riches when other people don't? The problem, of course, with that argument is that you can't help anyone if you have nothing to help them with. You help others by giving, leading by example and inspiring them to fulfill their potential.

"Our subconscious beliefs are very powerful," reiterated Mr. Appleby. "They influence everything in our lives. One of the best truisms in life was first stated by Clement Stone, one of the greatest entrepreneurs of the twentieth century. Here it is," he said showing the young man a plaque which had an inscription: 'Whatever the mind can conceive and believe, it can achieve.'"

"I understand what you're saying," said the young man. "But I can't imagine that it is easy to change your subconscious beliefs."

Mr. Appleby smiled. "That in itself is a prime example of a disempowering, negative belief. Do you know for certain that it is difficult to change your subconscious beliefs?"

"Well . . . no, but . . . "

"Always remember those words of Clement Stone, 'Whatever the mind can conceive and believe it can achieve.' You have the power to choose your beliefs."

"How?" asked the young man.

"Autosuggestion," said Mr. Appleby.

"What's that?" asked the young man.

"Autosuggestion is simply a technique in which you repeatedly make suggestions to yourself."

"How is something you suggest to yourself going to influence your subconscious beliefs?" asked the young man.

"Any statement or suggestion you repeat often enough, will eventually enter your subconscious," explained Mr. Appleby. "After all, this was how you learned most of your beliefs in the first place. You heard them being spoken over and over again, and eventually they entered your subconscious and you believed them."

The young man jotted down some notes as Mr. Appleby continued. "What you need to do is to create positive associations or beliefs about money and wealth through autosuggestion. The first thing to do is to turn the old negative beliefs around; instead of saying, 'Money doesn't grow on trees,' which is a statement implying that money is scarce and that you will never have much of it, rather say, 'Yes, money doesn't grow on trees, it grows out of my determined and planned efforts.' Instead of saying, 'Money can't bring happiness,' say, 'Money may not be able to bring happiness, but lack of money never did either!' Or change 'Money is the root of all evil' to 'Love of money is the root of all

22

evil, but in the right hands money is a source of great blessing.'"

"Then add your own positive suggestions such as; 'Wealth brings power, freedom and security,' 'I am capable of creating abundant wealth.' In this way you will start to change your subconscious beliefs about yourself and about money and wealth."

The young man looked up from his notepad. "How often do you need to repeat these autosuggestions?" he asked.

"As often as possible," replied Mr. Appleby. "And at least three times a day—once before you get out of bed, once during the day and another time before bed."

The young man scribbled down notes so as not to forget.

"Whatever you believe you can do," said Mr. Appleby, "is very often what you will do. It's like this poem here," he said, pointing to a framed piece of prose on his desk. The poem read:

If you think you're beaten, you are.
If you think you dare not, you don't.
If you like to win, but you think you can't,
It is almost certain you won't.

If you think you'll lose, you're lost,
For out in the world we find,
Success begins with a fellow's will—
It's all in the state of mind.

If you think you are outclassed, you are,
You've got to think high to rise,
You've got to be sure of yourself before
You can ever win a prize.

Life's battles don't always go
To the stronger or faster man,
But soon or late the man who wins
Is the man who thinks he can!

Anon.

"That's an inspiring poem," said the young man. "Do you mind if I write it down?"

"With pleasure." Mr. Appleby smiled. "And you might also like this quote by Ralph Waldo Emerson," he said, passing a card to the young man. "This was my first autosuggestion and I keep it with me all the time to remind me of what is attainable." On the back of the card was written:

They conquer, who believe they can!

That night the young man read over the notes he had made of his meeting with Mr. Appleby:

The first secret of Abundant Wealth—the power of subconscious beliefs.

People do not achieve what they are capable of but what they *believe* they are capable of.

All of our circumstances in life are a reflection of our subconscious beliefs.

People generally earn exactly what they believe they are worth.

We can change our subconscious beliefs through autosuggestion.

Whatever our minds can conceive and believe, we can achieve!

Those who conquer, believe they can!

The
POWER
of a
BURNING
DESIRE

The following day the young man traveled to a small village 60 km north of the city to meet the second person on his list, a man by the name of Rupert Cummings. After an hour's journey, he finally arrived at the entrance to the grounds of a large country estate. As he walked up the pebbled driveway, he couldn't help but be impressed by the magnificence of the gardens. The front lawn which he estimated stretched for at least 500m was as immaculately mown as a putting green. There was a large cedar tree in the middle of the lawn surrounded by clusters of daffodils, and around the periphery of the garden were perfectly cut hedges amid borders filled with purples and golds of lobelia blossom and marigold flowers.

The driveway led to a circle in front of the house and in its center was a lily pond with a fountain sculpted into the shape of three dolphins. The house itself was wrapped in clematis which was beginning to show an array of pink buds, the first sign of an early spring. Just as the young man approached the end of the driveway a man, dressed in denim dungarees and wearing a large Australian bush hat and sunglasses, emerged from a path to the side of the house pushing a wheelbarrow. He was a tall man with a rich, silver-gray beard hiding an otherwise pale complexion. As he reached the young man he removed his sunglasses, revealing clear, cobalt colored eyes.

"Can I help you?" he called to the young man.

"I'm here to see Mr. Cummings," replied the young man. "I believe he is expecting me."

"Indeed I am. How do you do?" said the man, offering his hand to the young man.

"Er . . . fine . . . thank you," stuttered the young man shaking Mr. Cummings's hand.

"It's such a beautiful day. Do you mind if we sit outside?" asked Mr. Cummings.

"Not at all," said the young man.

Mr. Cummings led the young man along the path to the back of the house and as he entered the back garden his eyes met with breathtaking scenery. If the front lawns were beautiful, the grounds to the rear of the house were simply majestic. There was a gravel path leading down the center of the lawns, lined on either side by evergreens. The lawns themselves were surrounded by flowerbeds filled with an assortment of bright colors.

The two men sat down at a white-enameled cast iron table which was set on a large terrace overlooking the garden. Within minutes a butler came toward them carrying a tray.

"Would you like some tea?" Mr. Cummings asked the young man.

"Thank you. That would be fine," replied the young man.

As Mr. Cummings poured the tea, the young man briefly told him about his meeting with the old Chinese man.

"The secrets of Abundant Wealth?" said Mr. Cummings.

"Yes, of course I know of them. All that I have, I have acquired through the secrets."

"Which secrets in particular?" asked the young man.

"They are all equally important and they all helped me get where I am today, but the secret that, looking back, I think that I most needed to learn was the power of a burning desire."

"Desire?" repeated the young man. "But surely everybody desires to be wealthy?"

"You'd think so wouldn't you," replied Mr. Cummings, "but, in actual fact, very few people have a desire to be wealthy, never mind a burning desire."

"I don't know about that," said the young man. "Why would someone not want to be wealthy?"

"Let's start from the beginning," said Mr. Cummings. "Human beings are motivated by only one of two things—pain or pleasure. If we think something will give us pleasure we want it and if we think it will bring us pain, we avoid it. You agree?"

The young man nodded. "I suppose so," he said. "But being wealthy brings pleasure, doesn't it?"

"Yes. It does. Or rather it can. But many people think that having money or wealth will bring pain. You already found out about the power of our subconscious beliefs?"

The young man nodded but this time remained silent.

"So you know that some people believe that having money will bring pain of sorts. For example, some people think that their friends will change toward them, or they worry about the responsibility of having wealth. Sometimes they worry about taxes or people making demands from them.

"Deep down, people who have these fears don't really have a desire for wealth, certainly not Abundant Wealth. And so, they live without it.

"What it boils down to," explained Mr. Cummings, "is that if you want Abundant Wealth you have to associate more pleasure with acquiring it and having it than living without it. You have to want it, more than want it, you have to have a burning desire for it. You have got to desire it so much that you will be willing to make whatever sacrifices are necessary (excluding sacrifices to your health, your personal relationships and your integrity) to overcome any obstacle that stands in your way.

"That is why no person who tries to quit smoking, no alcoholic who tries to stay sober and no dieter who tries to lose weight can ever succeed until they desire it so badly that they are willing to change. If you are going to achieve anything in life, you have got to have a burning desire.

"When I met the old Chinese man, fifteen years ago, I was about to be made bankrupt and lose everything I had. I owned a gas station on one of the main highways out of the city. It did well too. So well that I was able to build a restaurant attached to it. Everything was going wonderfully and I was doing very nicely, until a new, bigger highway was opened three kilometers eastward. Almost overnight, the traffic passing my garage plummeted. Revenues fell and within six months the situation was hopeless. There was no way in the world that I would be able to get sufficient revenue to pay the overheads, let alone make any profit. I had sunk everything I owned into that business and, from being a relatively wealthy man, I found myself over sixty years old and virtually penniless!"

The young man looked up with raised eyebrows from his notepad. "You had to start over again when you were over sixty years of age?" he said.

"Yes. I did," nodded Mr. Cummings.

"But most people are getting ready to retire at that

age," exclaimed the young man. "What on earth did you do?"

"At the time, I had no idea. All I knew is that I had to do something. I was sitting in my restaurant one day when a little old Chinese man walked in. He sat down opposite me on the adjacent table and said, 'Good morning.' He was a very friendly chap and we seemed to hit it off immediately. He had the speciality of the house—my own special deep-fried spiced potato chips—and complimented me on how good they were. It was the one thing that everyone who ever ate in the restaurant used to love. When he finished the meal he asked why the place was so empty and I explained about the new highway. He asked me what I was going to do and I told him I didn't know. I had worked for the best part of twenty years building up the gas station and the restaurant. Up until the opening of the new highway, business was flourishing but what could you do if traffic was no longer passing by?

"The old man looked at me quite solemnly and said, 'In my country, we believe that in every adversity lies the seed of an equivalent or greater benefit.' I said, 'You must be joking. What possible benefit could there be in losing what had taken me over twenty years to build up?' And he said, 'Because there are greater things waiting for you. When one door closes, you have to open another. You can have anything you want in life . . . if you want it badly enough and are prepared to do whatever it takes to get it.'

"I looked out of the window, contemplating what I was going to do and what possible good could come from my situation. I had turned away for a moment, no longer, but when I turned back toward the old man he was gone. At the table he had left payment for his meal and a piece of paper containing a list of ten names and telephone numbers followed by a message, 'Thanks for the meal. Those deep-fried potato chips were delicious!'"

Mr. Cummings took a sip of tea before continuing his story. "I called the people on the old man's list just to try and find out more about him, but instead learned about the secrets of Abundant Wealth. As I said, I was in a desperate situation and so I was ready to give anything a go."

"And the secrets helped you?" asked the young man.

"Well, take a look around you." Mr. Cummings smiled. "Without the secrets of Abundant Wealth, I would be either dead or surviving on state benefits now."

"Are you serious?" asked the young man.

"Of course," replied Mr. Cummings.

"So, how exactly did having a burning desire help you?" asked the young man.

"It made me determined to succeed," answered Mr. Cummings. "You can't achieve anything worthwhile in life unless you have a burning desire for it, because achievement requires effort, determination and commitment. I had always had a desire to be comfortable, but after losing my business I had a burning desire not just to be wealthy, but to be massively wealthy to prove to myself and to other people that I could do it. People told me that I was too old to start over, that I was foolish to try and should make the best of what I had.

"And that was it, I decided to make the best of what I had and use it to create wealth."

"What did you have?" asked the young man.

"A recipe for deep-fried spiced potato chips!" exclaimed Mr. Cummings.

"You're joking," said the young man. "What good is a recipe for potato chips?"

Mr. Cummings smiled. "I reckoned it would be of value for restaurants and cafés. I knew it was a popular recipe—everyone who ever ate in my restaurant loved them—so I traveled around the country trying to sell my recipe. I offered to give my recipe to restaurants for no payment other than a small percentage of the increased sales in potato chips made with my recipe. Most restaurant managers laughed at me. 'What do we need your recipe for?' they would say. 'We've got our own.' 'But my recipe is special,' I argued. Most wouldn't even taste my potato chips but I persisted because I had a burning desire to succeed. I visited over a thousand restaurants before someone finally agreed to try my recipe. Three years later I had five contracts and within another four years I had a business that made me a multimillionaire. I was nearly seventy years old, but I did it. So you see, the old Chinese man was right—losing my gas station proved to be the best thing that ever happened to me."

The young man grinned. "You can say that again!"

"Have you ever read *A Christmas Carol* by Charles Dickens?" Mr. Cummings asked.

"Yes," replied the young man.

"What made Scrooge change his ways?"

"The Ghosts of Christmas Past, Present, and Future," said the young man.

"Yes, but how did they make him change?"

"Erm . . . they showed him what would happen if he didn't change," answered the young man.

"That's right. The Ghost of Christmas Past showed him the pain he had suffered by being mean-spirited and miserly, the Ghost of Christmas Present highlighted the pain he was suffering in the present and the Ghost of Christmas Future revealed what pain would be in store if he didn't change. Consequently, when Scrooge woke up and found he was still alive, he decided to change his ways.

"And we can use the same principles that the three Ghosts used for Scrooge to make changes in our own lives, whether it be to change our financial status, our career or even our relationships. We need to desire the change. We must identify the pain with not changing and appreciate the pleasure we will gain if we do change. This is the only way to produce a strong motivation to do the things necessary to succeed in making the changes we want in our lives.

"And the only way we can create such a desire is by using a similar approach as was used by the Christmas Ghosts for Scrooge. It is a simple four-step process. The first step is to remember all of the pain of the past that was caused as a result of the condition that you want to change. So, if the change required is to make more money, the pain of the past might be recalled by remembering all of those times when you wanted to buy loved ones things that you simply couldn't afford."

Images came into the young man's mind; in his childhood of being teased for wearing old worn-out, hand-me-down clothes while his friends wore the latest fashions. Memories of all the times at college when he had been unable to go out with his friends because he had no spare money and the attractive red-haired girl at college who he dared not ask out because he didn't have a car. But, the one most painful memory came later when his mother needed expensive dental work which she couldn't afford and he had been unable to help her. Lack of money had caused a lot of pain in his past.

The young man's thoughts were interrupted as Mr. Cummings continued.

"The second step is to consider all of the pain in your life at the moment that is being caused by the condition that you want to change. In my case, there was a lot of pain. I was losing everything I had worked for."

The young man knew only too well the present pain his lack of finances was creating in his life. He had had many sleepless nights over it. But he had never thought of the pain and anguish as helping him improve his life.

"The third step," explained Mr. Cummings, "is to imagine all of the pain you will experience in the future if you don't change. The pain of not being able to afford to buy the special present that your children want on their birthday or the pain of not being able to pay for your children to go to college or university. Not being able to take proper care of your family. Or perhaps the thought of never being able to be in a position to help friends and family, or never being able to afford a house large enough to have friends visit you."

The young man tried to imagine being married with children. Not being able to provide for them would be so awful that he didn't even want to think about it. He took a deep breath; the past, present and future seemed to form nothing but pain.

"Isn't this all a bit depressing?" he asked. "Why focus on all of the pain in your life?"

"It is negative," admitted Mr. Cummings, "but if it creates a burning desire to change your life, then it's worth it, wouldn't you say?"

The young man nodded. "Yes, but . . . "

"The anxiety and pain we experience when struggling to pay our bills, or having no savings for emergencies, or being unable to afford things for ourselves or our family and friends can provide the impetus we need to change our lives," explained Mr. Cummings. "Remember, if you want to change your life, you have got to create a burning desire to change it. The three steps I have just mentioned are the 'stick'—the pain that you want to avoid. The fourth and final step is the carrot. This time you have to imagine all of the pleasure you'll get in the future by having Abundant Wealth. The pleasure of being able to buy those things you have always dreamed of—perhaps a bigger house, a car, holidays; the joy of being able to give to and help the people you love, or the satisfaction of being able to support a particular charity.

"But, when I say 'imagine,' I mean you've got to really visualize these things, see them happening in your mind so that you can experience in your imagination what it will actually feel like not to be able to afford certain things in the future and what it will feel like if you accumulate the resources to satisfy your needs and desires.

"That way," continued Mr. Cummings, "you'll develop a burning desire for Abundant Wealth. And, as soon as you have a burning desire for anything, Life soon presents a way for you to obtain it."

"You really believe that?" asked the young man. "If you desire something firmly enough, Life will present you with a way to obtain it?"

"Of course," answered Mr. Cummings. "Do you know where the Latin root of the word 'desire' comes from?"

The young man shook his head.

"'De'—of, 'sire'—father . . . 'of the father.' You have been given the ability to choose whatever your heart desires, and with that choice is also given the ability to fulfill those desires. In other words, you would not have a desire without also having been given the power to create it in your life."

"I see," said the young man. "So what you're saying is that anything you want badly enough, you have the power to get."

"Precisely. And I'm living proof. If a man over sixty years of age like me can do it, believe me, anyone can!"

That night, before going to bed, the young man summarized the notes he had made:

The second secret of Abundant Wealth—the power of desire.

If you don't have Abundant Wealth in your life it generally means that you don't yet have a burning desire for Abundant Wealth.

You can't attain anything worthwhile in life without a burning desire for its attainment.

You have a burning desire only when you are willing to do whatever it takes and make whatever sacrifices are necessary (excluding sacrificing your self-respect, your health or your relationships).

You can create a burning desire using the approach of the three Christmas ghosts:

- remember the pain of the past caused by your lack of money.
- think of all the present pain caused by your lack of money.
- think of all the pain there will be in the future if your present financial circumstances don't change.
- imagine all of the pleasure you will have in the future if you have wealth in abundance!

The
POWER
of
DEFINITENESS
OF PURPOSE

The following week the young man traveled into the heart of the city to meet the third person on his list, a man by the name of Michael Chapman. Mr. Chapman was president of an international communications corporation. He was an imposing figure of a man, tall and lean, immaculately dressed in a dark gray pinstriped, double-breasted suit, white cotton shirt and a plain gray tie. He looked to be fairly young—in his mid-forties—with neatly trimmed brown hair and large hazel eyes.

After the young man had told Mr. Chapman about his meeting with the old Chinese man and his two subsequent meetings, Mr. Chapman sat back in his chair and drew his fingers together as if in deep contemplation.

"Tell me something," he said to the young man. "What do you want to attain in your life?"

"Excuse me, sir?" asked the young man, taken back by Mr. Chapman's directness.

"What do you want from life?" repeated Mr. Chapman.

"Erm . . . all I want is . . . to be happy . . . healthy . . . and, of course, prosperous," replied the young man. "Doesn't everybody?"

"Yes. And that is precisely the reason why so few people are healthy, happy or prosperous!"

"What do you mean?"

"If you don't know what you are looking for in life, how will you ever find it?"

"But I just said what I wanted—to be healthy, happy and prosperous," insisted the young man.

"But these terms are vague, general, non-specific descriptions. What do you mean by them?"

"I'm sorry," spluttered the young man, "but I don't understand."

"Well, let's take the term prosperous, as that is what you're here for; what do you need to have in order to feel prosperous? How much would you need to earn before you felt prosperous?"

"Oh . . . I see," said the young man, finally understanding what was being asked. "To feel prosperous, I would have to earn at least twice my present salary."

"Okay, that's a start. Anything else?" asked Mr. Chapman.

"I would have to own a house, free from a mortgage, a car . . . "

"What type of house and car?" interrupted Mr. Chapman.

"I don't know," replied the young man. "It's not important."

"Really?" said Mr. Chapman. "So a one-bedroomed house in one of the city's slum areas would be acceptable?"

"No, of course not," said the young man.

"Then what sort of house would it have to be?" asked Mr. Chapman.

"I would say a five-bedroomed house in a northern suburb on the outskirts of the city."

"Now you're getting somewhere," said Mr. Chapman.

"Do you think you would be able to afford to buy such a house if you earned twice your present salary?" he asked.

"No," laughed the young man. "I would need to earn ten times my salary to afford such a house."

"In that case why did you just say that you would feel prosperous if you earned twice your present salary?"

"I . . . I suppose I hadn't really thought it through," admitted the young man.

"Can you see the contradictions?" asked Mr. Chapman. "Many people say that they want to be wealthy, but very few take the time to consider what it is they really want, or why they want it. If you want to start to create Abundant Wealth in your life, you will have to think these things through. It is absolutely essential to find out exactly what it is you want and need, down to the last detail. It's no good saying, for example, that you want a new car. You need to know the exact make, model and color because only then can your mind have something to focus on. And on top of having specific goals you also need to know the reasons why you want them or how achieving your goals will benefit you.

"In my youth," continued Mr. Chapman, "I thought I could beat the system; I didn't need qualifications, I wasn't interested in studying; all I was concerned about was having a good time. But I soon found out that I couldn't get a decent job because I had no qualifications. Looking back it seems so ridiculous, and for a time I put the blame on my schooling. I should have been told how important it was to study and get qualifications, but the truth was that I had been told, only I hadn't listened.

"I didn't know what I wanted to do with my life. I became despondent and depressed and very bitter. Why should other people have new cars, big homes, designer clothes and exotic holidays when I couldn't have them? I didn't stop to think that other people had those things because they put in the time and effort to get them, whereas I had squandered my youth. I blamed everybody—my parents, my teachers, even the government—but there was only one person to blame and that was myself.

"One day I was left a small bequest by an old aunt and went down to the travel agent to see about booking a holiday—to get away from it all for two weeks. I took the brochures to the park and began to look through them to select a holiday.

"The next thing I knew, an old Chinese man was sitting beside me. He asked me if I was going somewhere nice and I explained that I wasn't sure where I was going to go. I only knew that I was getting away for a few weeks. Then he asked me why I wanted to get away and so I told him I had no job, no prospects and no future. Then he turned to me and looked me squarely in the eye and said, 'Then you must create a future.'"

"How can you create your own future?" interrupted the young man.

"That's exactly what I asked," said Mr. Chapman, "and the old man simply said 'Through the secrets of Abundant Wealth.' Then he gave me a list of people who he said would be able to explain them to me."

The young man smiled to himself.

"And it was through those people," explained Mr. Chapman, "that I discovered that one of my biggest problems was that I had no goals, no direction and consequently no purpose in my life. I learned that I could have anything that I wanted, anything at all, but I would first have to know exactly what it was that I wanted and why I wanted it. This is the power of having definiteness of purpose."

"Definiteness of purpose," repeated the young man as

he made some notes in his notepad. "So you're saying that we need to have goals to create wealth," he said.

"Well, goals are the first part, yes," acknowledged Mr. Chapman. "You have to have specific goals. It is no good simply saying I would like to be wealthy. To build a future you have to focus on what you would like to have and the specific time by which you would like to have it."

"How does that help you acquire wealth, though?" asked the young man.

"Imagine that you set off on a journey, but you have no destination in mind. Where will you end up?" replied Mr. Chapman.

The young man smiled. "That's anybody's guess," he said.

"Precisely. No one knows. You could go off in any direction at any time depending upon how you feel at any moment. But if you have a fixed destination before you set off, where are you most likely to end up?"

"I see . . . at the destination point," said the young man.

"Of course. Life is like a journey; if you know where you want to go, you're more likely to get there."

The young man made some more notes. He had never had specific goals before, but he could now see their value.

"Having goals is only one part of the process of developing definiteness of purpose. Let's go back to our imaginary journey and say you have a number of destinations you would like to visit. How can you make absolutely sure that you visit them all?"

"Write them down?"

"Very good. That is why, to be most effective, goals have to be written down and referred to regularly so that you can check you are going in the right direction. It's like going to the supermarket; if you go without a shopping list, you might set out knowing what you want, but as you go round the aisles you'll become distracted by the marketing and advertising and the general commotion in the store, and chances are that you'll come away without some of the important things you needed."

The young man laughed. "That happens to me all the time. I'm always coming out of a supermarket without some of the things I specifically went in for and with other things that I didn't set out to buy and probably didn't need."

"Now, if you had a shopping list, that wouldn't happen. Because as you pass through the supermarket you would refer to the list and know precisely what to buy."

"It sounds so simple," said the young man.

"It is," answered Mr. Chapman, smiling.

"So you're saying it is more effective to write your goals down?" asked the young man.

"Yes. And refer to them every day, preferably three times a day so that they are always on your mind. That way, you will always be focused on where you are headed and most of the things you do will be related to the achievement of those goals. Whatever you choose to do will be determined by your goals. If, for instance, you have a goal to finish a certain project by the end of the week, you will spend your spare time completing the project rather than, say, watching television.

"To be most effective your goals have to be phrased in such a way that they trigger your subconscious mind," said Mr. Chapman.

"What exactly do you mean?" asked the young man.

"Well, how are goals usually phrased? How do people usually express, for example, their new year's resolutions? They say, 'I hope to . . . ,' 'I am going to . . . ,' 'I will try to. . . .' These phrases don't work and that is why most people don't stick to their new year's resolutions," explained Mr. Chapman.

"What's wrong with them?" asked the young man.

"Well, if someone says that they are *going to* give up smoking, do you think they will succeed?"

The young man shrugged his shoulders.

"You can bet your bottom dollar that they won't," said Mr. Chapman, "because the day someone is serious about quitting cigarettes, he or she says, "I am a non-smoker.""

"Have you heard the example of a hypnotist who makes a person lie with their head supported by one chair and their feet supported by another with nothing in the middle to support them?"

"Yes, I have," answered the young man.

"Imagine what would happen if the hypnotist said to one of his subjects, 'You *might be* as straight as a board. We are *going to try* and make you become as rigid as a piece of steel.' That man will be wide awake running back to his seat. What the hypnotist does say is, 'You *are* as straight as a board, as rigid as a piece of steel.' No 'going to be,' 'perhaps' or 'maybe.' No 'trying to' or 'hope for.' The hypnotist uses a positive statement expressed in the present tense.

"And the same applies to the way we express our goals. Instead of 'I would like to . . . ,' or 'I will try to . . . ' or 'I hope to earn $150,000 by December 31 of this year,' state instead, 'I am earning $150,000 between now and December 31 of this year.' Always remember when writing your goals—make them *positive* affirmations stated in the *present* tense.

"If you write down your goals in this way you are halfway to achieving them. There is something almost magical about writing down your goals in positive and present statements that actually draws them into your life. Simply by putting them on paper and reading them three times a day—morning, afternoon and evening—starts the process of acquiring them."

"Really?" asked the young man.

"Well, all I can say is try it and see what happens," answered Mr. Chapman. "Written goals are extremely powerful in determining your achievements in life. Once you have written them down, see yourself achieving them."

"What do you mean?" asked the young man.

"It's a process called creative visualization. Whatever your goals are, imagine yourself already acquiring them. If, for example, one of your goals is to live in a certain house, see yourself living there. Or if your goal is to get a particular job, see yourself in that job."

"But isn't that just wishful thinking?" protested the young man.

"You know a wise old man once told me: 'If you wish it, it is no dream.' When you imagine yourself already achieving your goals, the goals become more real, more possible. It is a technique used by all of the greatest athletes and sportsmen and -women because it induces a feeling of confidence, a feeling of certainty that you can and will achieve your goals."

"Okay," said the young man. "So you have to identify your goals, write them down and visualize yourself achieving them."

"Yes. But there is one additional thing that makes the process of having goals even more powerful, and that is identifying the reasons why you want or need those goals."

"Why is that?" asked the young man.

"Because reasons give the goals purpose. For example; to have a goal of earning a certain sum of money is not as powerful a motivation as having a goal to earn a certain sum of money in order to afford a particular apartment or a special holiday, or to be able to send your children to college. Whatever it is, you need purpose.

After all, what will motivate you more, the goal of acquiring $15,000 or the goal of acquiring $15,000 to put down as a deposit with which to purchase your own home? Remember that wealth is not about accumulating money and possessions for their own sake, but the power it will give you to fulfill your purpose or purposes in life. Identifying the reasons behind your goals creates the unstoppable power of definiteness of purpose."

That evening the young man read over the notes he had made:

The third secret of Abundant Wealth—the power of definiteness of purpose.

You can have anything you want in Life provided you know exactly what you want and why you want it.

You must be specific about your goals, the reasons why you must achieve those goals and the time by which you must achieve them. (For example, it is not sufficient to say that you want to be wealthy. You must state the exact amount of money you wish to acquire, the possessions you want to own, and the things you want to do.)

Always phrase your goals positively in the present tense. (For example, "I *am* earning [X amount of dollars] between now and [insert the date you have set to achieve it]).

Write down your goals and read them three times a day—morning, afternoon, and evening.

Visualize yourself achieving your goals.

Identify the reasons why you must achieve your goals.

Remember wealth is not about accumulating money or possessions for their own sake, but the power it will give you to fulfill your purpose or purposes in life.

The POWER *of an* ORGANIZED PLAN OF ACTION

"So, you have written out your goals, expressed them positively in the present tense; you have set a time by which you want to achieve your goals and identified the reasons why it is important that you achieve them. Now you have definiteness of purpose—you know what you want, why you want it and when you want it by—but what next?"

The young man was sitting opposite Erika Hill, editor-in-chief of a large, international publishing company and the fourth person on his list. When he met Mrs. Hill, the young man was surprised at her youthful appearance. He had expected someone of her position to be middle-aged, but Mrs. Hill was only 39 years of age and looked ten years younger still. She was an attractive woman with long, auburn hair and bright green eyes and, despite having had three children, she had managed to retain a slim figure.

"To tell you the truth," answered the young man, "I have no idea. I mean, you're right, I know my goals but I don't know how I will ever achieve them."

"That's all right," said Mrs. Hill. "Twelve years ago, I was in exactly the same position. I started my career as a freelance journalist and I managed to continue working through my pregnancies and while bringing up my children. In fact, I wrote about issues related to young mothers and families, the things that interested me at the time. That meant that whenever we did something as a family, I would normally find something to write about. I sold most of my articles to magazines and newspapers and made quite a good living considering I was also bringing up three children, but I had bigger dreams—what I really wanted was to run my own magazine. The only problem was that it always seemed like a pipe dream because it would need such a large amount of capital to set up.

"Then one day I was traveling up north to do an interview and found myself sitting opposite an old Chinese man who was traveling to the same city. He was a very friendly sort and we talked for most of the journey. At one point, I told him that I was a journalist and had dreams of one day owning my own magazine although I confessed that it would probably never happen because it would require a lot of money.

"He leaned forward, touched my arm and said, 'If you will it, it is no dream.'"

"What does that mean?" asked the young man.

"I asked the same question," said Mrs. Hill, "and the old man said, 'whatever your mind can conceive and believe, it can achieve.'"

The young man recalled how the old man had given him the same advice and began to jot down some notes.

"It was then that the old man mentioned the secrets of Abundant Wealth," continued Mrs. Hill. "He gave me the names and phone numbers of ten people who he said would be able to explain the secrets to me. I went to see them all, if nothing else because I thought it might make a good story, but I soon discovered that they really did work. And, the one secret that had a tremendous impact on my life was the power of an organized plan of action."

"What do you mean by that exactly?" asked the young man.

"Well, knowing what you want and why you want it is important, and sometimes that alone will attract your goals into your life, but if you want to make certain that you will achieve your goals you have got to develop a strategy to work toward them. That means making an organized plan of action.

"All successful athletes plan their future. They plot out a training schedule to try and ensure that they peak just in time for the major events. Two weeks before or after an event isn't good enough. They need to peak at the event if they are going to give their best. And the same is true in life; there is not one millionaire who earned his or her fortune without first drawing up and following an organized plan of action. In fact, years ago, I asked a very successful and wealthy businessman what was the secret of his success, and he told me that to succeed in anything you needed to do three things: Get organized . . . get organized . . . and get organized! And there is a lot of sense in that advice. Can you imagine trying to build a house without architect's plans? What materials and equipment would it need? Where would you lay the foundations? What shape would you build it and how many stories high? Without a plan, you wouldn't know where to start."

The young man nodded in agreement.

"Well, the same principles apply whatever you want to build, be it a house, a boat, a car . . . or wealth. It needs an organized plan of action.

"Instead of just trying to make a living, if we draw up an organized plan of action, we can design the life we want to live. It is crucial even in small matters; let's say, for example, that your television is broken and you need a new one. You know the make and model of the one you want to get. The next question is, 'what will you have to do to get it?'"

"You just need to find out what shops sell it and go and buy it," said the young man.

"Okay. You find out where it is sold. But what happens if it is too expensive?"

"Then you can't buy it. Simple," answered the young man.

"Did the old man mention the golden rule of problem solving to you?" asked Mrs. Hill.

The young man thumbed through his notebook and found the page he was looking for. "'When you think you have exhausted all possibilities, remember one thing . . . you haven't,'" he read from the page.

"Exactly!" replied Mrs. Hill. "There is always a way. You just need to find it. So let's say the television costs $300 and you only have $150 spare. What can you do to get your television?"

"Well, you could wait. Invest the $150 and save the other hundred. $15 a month over ten months and you'll be able to buy it."

"Yes. That's a possibility. But you would be without a television for ten months. Is there anything else you could do?"

"I suppose you could borrow or buy it on credit."

"That's another possibility, but you might have to pay high interest charges if you can't pay it off quickly."

"That's all I can think of," said the young man.

"Okay. What about asking if they will accept an offer? Most shops put high mark-ups on their goods and you would be surprised how many would be willing to make a sale for less than the asking price. Or you could ask if they will accept interest-free credit. They may even accept your old television as a trade in. You see there are always options. Things may seem impossible at first glance, but when you sit down and make an organized plan of action, you will begin to see that there are, in fact, many possibilities.

"All you need is to create a ten-point plan of action. Jot down ten possibilities."

"Can you give me an example?" said the young man.

"Certainly. In my case I needed to raise $150,000 to start my own magazine. So I wrote out ten possibilities:

1. Find a person or company to invest $150,000.
2. Find two investors, each to invest $75,000.
3. Find five investors, each to invest $30,000.
4. Find ten investors, each to invest $15,000.
5. Find twenty investors, each to invest $7,500.
6. Find fifty investors, each to invest $3,000.
7. Find one hundred investors each to invest $1,500.
8. Find two hundred investors, each to invest $750.
9. Borrow some money from a bank.
10. Sell the idea to an established publishing company who would publish the magazine in partnership with me.

"The whole project didn't look so impossible at all once I had made a list of possibilities. Now, I do a ten-point plan for every project, every goal I have."

"I see, and does it work for all your goals?" asked the young man.

"Definitely, because it makes you explore different ways of achieving your goals that you may not have considered before. I once read a story about an American priest who wanted to begin a new church in a new town. He had no money to build a church and so he sat down and began making a ten-point plan. He wrote down:

1. Rent a school building.
2. Rent a Masonic hall.
3. Rent an Elk's lodge.
4. Rent a mortuary chapel.
5. Rent an empty warehouse.
6. Rent a community club building.
7. Rent a Seventh-Day Adventist church.
8. Rent a Jewish synagogue.
9. Rent a drive-in theater.
10. Rent an empty piece of ground, a tent and folding chairs.

"All of a sudden he had ten possibilities and he went on to set up his church in a drive-in theater. Years later, and with an established congregation, Dr. Robert Schuller had a dream of building a cathedral with a steeple so tall, it would be seen from all over the county. It would be called the 'Tower of Hope' and serve not only as a place of prayer and learning as well as a community center, but it would be a source of hope and inspiration for the whole county. There was, however, one snag, it would cost a million dollars. People told Dr. Schuller that it was an impossible task, but once again he used the ten-point plan:

1. Get one person to give $1,000,000.
2. Get 2 people to give $500,000.
3. Get 4 people to give $250,000.
4. Get 10 people to give $100,000.
5. Get 20 people to give $50,000.
6. Get 40 people to give $25,000.
7. Get 50 people to give $20,000.
8. Get 100 people to give $10,000.
9. Get 200 people to give $5,000.
10. Get 1,000 people to give $1,000.

"It took time to raise the money, but he did it! And, the ten-point plan he used can be used for any goal."

"Yes, I can see how this could help in a business situation," said the young man. "But what about in personal matters? One of my goals is to own a five-bedroomed house with two acres of grounds on the outskirts of the city. There is no way I could afford it on my current salary. I can barely afford a one-bedroomed apartment!"

"Well, that tells you something, doesn't it? Outside of winning the lottery, you'll have to find a way of increasing your income. That might mean aiming at promotion within your company or looking for a different job with better prospects. It may even mean seeking a change in career. But at least you now know that you have got to make some changes if you are going to be sure of achieving your goals.

"I know it seems daunting at first, but try doing the ten-point plan anyway. If you do it now, perhaps I can help you. Let's first think how you can increase your annual earnings. How much do you currently earn?"

"$22,500," answered the young man

"I see. So if you doubled your income each year, within five years you would be earning $720,000. More than enough to buy the house you want."

"Yes, but how do I double my income?" persisted the young man.

"Try the ten-point plan. Just write whatever ideas come into your head."

"Okay," said the young man. "I could work hard and get promoted to director level. I think they earn over $450,000 a year."

"That's one possibility, although perhaps a bit remote. It usually takes a lot more than five years to work up through the ranks of a company to directorship."

"The only other thing I could think of would be to get

a different job working on a commission so that my pay would be related to my sales."

"Yes. But it would have to be a very good commission," said Mrs. Hill. "What about getting more qualifications which will help you get a more highly paid job?"

"But I have commitments now. I need income," protested the young man.

"Yes, but you could go to night school."

"That's true," said the young man. "I hadn't thought of that."

"And what about starting up your own business?" suggested Mrs. Hill.

"That's a possibility as well," said the young man. "But what type of business?"

"Once again, organized planning will help you out. Many people end up in jobs without giving any thought to the kind of work they enjoy doing or what their personal strengths and weaknesses are. They give little or no consideration to what direction they want their careers to take. If this happens, the job is never more than just a means of earning a living. They will have no passion for what they do, there will be no interest or enthusiasm. Consequently, they will never become particularly good at their work and life will become a daily grind."

The young man took a deep breath. What Mrs. Hill was saying described his situation at work. He had no real interest in the work. The job was simply a means of paying his bills. He had never sat down and considered what sort of job he would enjoy doing or the type of work he was good at.

"These questions are essential," said Mrs. Hill, "if you want to do well, because unless you enjoy what you do and are good at what you do, it is very unlikely that your work will be well done. And if your work is not well done, how can you expect to be well paid?

"There is a very wise saying: Do what you love and the money will follow. If you love something, you're more likely to be willing to put in the effort to become good at it. Most people have this backward; they work to earn money to be able to do other things that they enjoy. Consequently, they spend five out of every seven days fed up in a job for which they have little interest and then wonder why they don't seem to be getting anywhere."

The young man knew that Mrs. Hill had described his feelings exactly.

"But how many people actually enjoy their work?" he insisted.

"Very few," answered Mrs. Hill, "but how many people are wealthy?"

"I take your point," he said. "So, what you're saying is that before applying for a job or starting up a business, you should really think about: 1) whether you enjoy the type of work, 2) whether it is suited to your particular talents, and 3) whether it will take you closer to your long-term career and financial goals."

"That's it." Mrs. Hill smiled.

"Well, I suppose it makes sense," said the young man. "I only wish I had thought about it years ago when I was still at college."

"You can't change the past," said Mrs. Hill. "But you can create your future. The question is, what are you going to do about it?"

"I don't know," said the young man. "That's why I'm here. I think that what I would really like to do is start up my own business."

"That's great. But what is the first thing you need to do?" asked Mrs. Hill.

"Draw up an organized plan of action?" answered the young man.

"Precisely!" exclaimed Mrs. Hill. "Any business needs

a business plan, a well thought-out, organized plan of action. If for any reason you needed to borrow money to fund your business, the first thing a potential investor will ask to see is a comprehensive business plan. They will want to see that you have thought everything through thoroughly because they know from experience that it is very unlikely any business will succeed if there is no organized plan of action directing it.

"That is why, if you want to create Abundant Wealth through any business venture, you have got to think your goals through and then plan what you are going to do and how you are going to do it."

Later that night the young man read through his notes:

The fourth secret of Abundant Wealth—the power of an organized plan of action.

If you want to be certain of achieving your goals, you have to develop a strategy, an organized plan of action.

Always remember the golden rule of problem solving—when you think you have exhausted all possibilities, remember one thing . . . you haven't.

If you want to succeed in anything, you must do three things—get organized . . . get organized . . . and get organized!

Use a ten-point plan for each of your goals, listing ten possible ways of achieving your goal.

Before accepting any job or starting any business—ask yourself three questions:

Will I enjoy the type of work?
Is it suited to my particular talents? and
Will it take me closer to my career goals and financial goals?

The
POWER
of
SPECIALIZED
KNOWLEDGE

Gloria Brown's was a remarkable, but true, story. Only seven years previously, she had been laid off. An administrative clerk working with computers in a small retail company, she had lost her job when the economy went into recession. With no real prospects of getting a job, she had found a way not only to survive, but to set up her own business which, within the first year, made her five times more than the salary she had been receiving as an office clerk.

Mrs. Brown looked to be in her mid- to late fifties. She was a petite woman, smartly dressed in a tartan suit which complimented her shoulder-length red hair and large, bright hazel eyes. But what the young man noticed most of all was her smile which appeared to be so warm and genuine that it literally seemed to light up her face.

The young man was eager to find out how Mrs. Brown had managed to make such a success out of such seemingly disastrous circumstances.

"If you want abundant wealth," she explained, "you have to learn to profit from every experience."

The young man recalled what the old Chinese man

had said to him: "Inside every adversity, every problem, is the seed of an equivalent or greater benefit." Could it really be true? he thought to himself.

"For the first few months of being unemployed," continued Mrs. Brown, "I wasn't quite that positive." She smiled. "In fact, I was thoroughly depressed about my situation because I couldn't see a way forward. But then I met the old Chinese man.

"My refrigerator had decided to break down and I called a repair service. A little old Chinese man turned up. I made him a cup of coffee as he examined my fridge and we began talking. I told him about my being laid off and he turned and looked up at me and said: 'If Life closes one door, you have to open another one.' It was then that he mentioned the secrets of Abundant Wealth to me. Naturally I was skeptical, but at the same time, I was curious. I was running out of savings, with no immediate prospects, and now no fridge. It was worth investigating. So, when he gave me a list of ten people who he said would be able to explain the powers of the secrets, I decided to contact them and find out more.

"And it was lucky I did, because they taught me the most important lesson I have ever learned in life, and that is that I am responsible for my own destiny. Whatever happens, whatever circumstances I face, I am responsible for my future and I have the power to create whatever future I desire."

The young man was becoming inspired listening to Mrs. Brown speak with such conviction and passion; there was no doubt that she sincerely believed in what she was saying.

"The one secret that had a particularly strong impression on me was the power of specialized knowledge," she said.

"So the old saying is true," said the young man, "Knowledge is power."

"No!" replied Mrs. Brown. "Knowledge is only *potential* power. It becomes power only when it is organized and intelligently applied through a practical plan of action toward a definite end."

The young man made notes as Mrs. Brown continued. "General knowledge has no value in the accumulation of wealth," she explained. "You can know trivia until it comes out of your ears, but it will not affect your potential to earn income or attract wealth one bit, unless of course you manage to get on a TV quiz show!

"Specialized knowledge, on the other hand, will always enable you to produce income. It doesn't matter what field of business you mention, if you don't have a specialized knowledge of the business, you will find it very difficult to succeed. It stands to reason, doesn't it; for example, if a friend were to ask you whether you would be prepared to invest in a new business he was starting, say, antique dealing, what would be the first question you would ask?"

"I would want to know what he knew about antiques and the antiques trade," replied the young man.

"Of course," replied Mrs. Brown. "Because you would know that the business wouldn't succeed unless your friend knew about the items he was buying and selling, and the markets they were sold in.

"But how often do we apply these questions to ourselves? We want to have money and the things it can buy, but how often do we think about the things we need to know about money? How much do we find out about taxes, investments or savings, all of which are vital subjects to know about if you want to create Abundant Wealth? If you don't have any knowledge of tax laws, for example, you could find yourself paying higher taxes than are necessary. Now, don't get me wrong, I'm not suggesting that you evade paying taxes, but I am saying that if you know and understand current tax laws—if you acquire that specialized knowledge—you can ensure that you don't pay more taxes than are absolutely necessary."

The young man jotted down some notes. He knew absolutely nothing about tax laws or investment schemes. It was something he would have to rectify, if nothing more than for peace of mind. Who knows, perhaps he would be able to find ways of legally reducing his tax bill.

"If you seek specialized knowledge you might also be able to reduce the amount you are paying on any debts," said Mrs. Brown.

"How is that?" asked the young man.

"One good example is credit card debts," explained Mrs. Brown. "Many people build up a debt on their credit cards and end up paying the very high interest rates charged by the credit card companies. They could reduce the interest payments by borrowing the sum required to clear the debt from a bank which will generally charge a much lower rate of interest. In this way, many people could significantly reduce their monthly interest charges."

"Really?" exclaimed the young man. "You mean to say that I could reduce the amount I am currently paying in monthly interest charges to credit card companies?"

"Of course," confirmed Mrs. Brown.

"That's unbelievable. What a fool I've been," he mumbled.

"Don't be too hard on yourself," said Mrs. Brown. "You can begin to see why specialized knowledge is so important though?"

"You bet!" said the young man.

"Specialized knowledge is equally important if you

want to get a highly paid job," continued Mrs. Brown. "If you want to earn a large salary, you have got to find out what those jobs are and what specialized knowledge you will need to obtain them. What qualifications are required and how you can go about getting those qualifications.

"Similarly, if you decide to start up a business of your own, you will need to make sure that you know all there is to know about the business."

"I understand what you're saying," said the young man, "but you can't know everything, can you?"

"That's true," answered Mrs. Brown. "I am not suggesting that you personally must have all the answers, but you need access to the answers. If you don't know about taxes, you need to employ a trustworthy accountant who does know about them; if you don't know about a product or service in your business, you need to work with somebody who does know, and if you don't know about an aspect of the business, let's say marketing, you need to employ somebody who is experienced and knows about marketing the type of products or services that you provide.

"Not even the best lawyer can know all there is to know about the law. There are just too many statutes and court rulings for a man to keep inside his head. And the laws are changing all the time. But a good lawyer knows where to find out about the laws."

"So what did you do to create your wealth?" asked the young man.

"I knew that I had to find another source of income, but the question was, what could I do? Or what did I have any specialized knowledge about? The answer was . . . very little and the little I did know was about computers. I had no real qualifications or specialized knowledge of any kind. But I knew then that if I was to create wealth, I would have to rectify that.

"I decided to go to night school and study computer technology. I reasoned that computers were going to become a vital part of all businesses and therefore a qualification in computer technology would be valuable to almost any business.

"It worked out well too. With just a small computer, a printer and a telephone I was able to start up a small consultancy business from my home. I called up a number of local businesses and found out whether they were using computers in their offices and if so, what they were using them for and any problems they were having."

The young man smiled. "I see . . . specialized knowledge of prospective customers and their needs," he said.

"Exactly. I discovered in what areas I could be of service. This is perhaps the most important area of specialized knowledge you need—knowledge of your prospective customers' needs. If you know what people want and need, you can succeed in any business. Too many people go into business focusing on what they have to offer, but the really successful businesses approach it from the viewpoint of the customer by first asking 'what does the customer want and need?' and then fulfilling their needs.

"After I found out what my prospective customers needed I was able to draw up proposals outlining ways in which my services could improve their efficiency and save them money. I could install hardware and prepare software computer programs specifically for their requirements, and I could show them how they could make better use of the computers that they were using. And, on top of it all, I could demonstrate that they would recoup my fees in administrative savings within less than a year. So, everybody was happy. And do you know who my first client was?"

The young man shook his head.

"The company that had fired me. I knew that they were struggling through the recession and I figured that I could cut their administrative costs by at least 25 percent through efficient use of specialized programs. My knowledge of how the company worked helped enormously and within six months of installing new computers and using the new software, the company had made a 35 percent savings on their costs. They were so impressed that they offered me an annual consultancy fee to do a review every year of their use of computers in administration.

"Within my first year I had 25 contracts and earned five times the earnings I had been making as an administrative clerk. The following year the business had grown to such a level that I had to employ other people and within three years I was grossing in excess of $1,500,000!

"So you can see that the old Chinese man was right when he told me that in every adversity was the seed of an equal or greater benefit. Had I not been laid off, I would not have retrained in computer technology and I would not be where I am today."

"And it was all down to specialized knowledge," said the young man.

"Specialized knowledge alone isn't a guarantee for success," said Mrs. Brown. "Remember that there are ten secrets of Abundant Wealth and they are all equally important. But no one who has ever accumulated wealth in abundance has done so without specialized knowledge . . . of tax laws, of investments and saving schemes, of their field of business, and their customers' wants and needs."

"Tell me something," said the young man before he left. "What was the name of the company that the old Chinese man worked for?"

"Why? You want to try and contact the old man?"

"Yes."

"I'm afraid I already tried to do that. Three months after I first met the old man, I called the head office to find out where he was."

"And where was he?"

"That's the strange thing," said Mrs. Brown. "The company had no record of a Chinese man ever having worked for them!"

That night the young man read over his notes:

The fifth secret of Abundant Wealth—the power of specialized knowledge.

No one who has ever accumulated wealth in abundance has done so without specialized knowledge ... of tax laws, of investments and saving schemes, of their field of business, and their customers' wants and needs.

Knowledge is power only when it is organized and intelligently applied through a practical plan of action toward a definite end.

You do not need to know everything yourself, but you do need to know where and how to find out about anything.

The POWER *of* PERSISTENCE

It wasn't until the following weekend that the young man was able to meet the sixth person on his list. Stuart Edgely was a famous actor. He had been working on location on the other side of the country, but was flying back to the city for the weekend and, on receiving the young man's message, agreed to meet him on Saturday morning at a small café in the city center.

The young man was excited and a little overawed about the prospect of meeting a celebrity, but when the day arrived, he found Mr. Edgely to be very personable and quite unassuming. In fact, he greeted the young man like a long-lost friend.

Despite being in his late thirties, Mr. Edgely looked like a man ten years his junior. He had jet-black hair and large puppy eyes surrounded by gold-rimmed round spectacles and was wearing a tanned bomber jacket over a cream turtleneck sweater and blue denim jeans.

"So you met the old Chinese man last week?" he asked the young man.

"Yes," answered the young man, who proceeded to relay the story of his meeting with the old Chinese man.

"I met him over twelve years ago. In this very café,"

confided Mr. Edgely. "And that one meeting with him changed my career and my life."

"In what way?" said the young man.

"Well, back then, my career was going through a slump. I hadn't had much work and was consequently waiting tables here to make ends meet. One day in walked a little old Chinese man and sat at the very same table we're sitting at now. It was the middle of the afternoon, a quiet time of the day. I asked him how he was and we soon began talking.

"I mentioned that I was an out-of-work actor and told him about the problems in the acting profession— too many people going for too few jobs in an underfunded industry. At any one time over ninety percent of the acting profession are either unemployed or doing a second job to help pay their way in between acting jobs.

"Then the old man said, 'you can't sit and wait for the right circumstances. You've got to go out and create them.'

"I told him, in my defense, that I had been on a number of casting sessions but I hadn't got anywhere. And then he looked up from his food and said, 'Then you have got to be like a stonecutter.' I asked him what he meant by that and he said: 'The stonecutter hammers away at a rock time and time again without so much as a crack appearing in it. But, if he persists, there will come a time when that rock will split wide open. It isn't one blow alone that breaks the rock, but the accumulation of many blows.'

"He said, 'If you want to crack the rock of success, you have to keep hammering away until it breaks.'

"'So,' I answered, 'you think that I should keep going up for jobs until I get one?' He nodded. 'Of course,' he said. 'The difference between people who succeed and those who don't is not necessarily talent, it is persistence!

Successful people begin their success where others end in failure.'"

"He then mentioned names of some film stars—Sylvester Stallone, Clint Eastwood, Sean Connery—all of whom had faced rejection early on in their careers. Sylvester Stallone was told he didn't speak well enough and he found it difficult even to get an agent to represent him. In the end he decided to write his own film in which he would take the lead role. He sent the manuscript to production companies but, one by one, they turned him down. But he never gave up. He persisted until one company said that they would make the film. But there was a condition . . . someone else would take the lead role. And even though at the time he was desperate for money, Sly Stallone stuck to his principles, he persisted and eventually it was agreed that he could take the lead role in the film *Rocky*. And the film that was turned down by numerous production companies went on to win an Oscar for Best Picture. So you see, Sylvester Stallone's success was not on account of his exceptional talent, but because he persisted.

"I was inspired by what the old man told me. I hadn't realized the importance of persistence—that even the superstars had been rejected in their careers. But I later discovered that not only had they experienced rejection, but some of them had suffered rejection on a huge scale. The old man then told me about the secrets of Abundant Wealth."

"What did you think about them?" asked the young man.

"I was skeptical at first," said Mr. Edgely, "but as I had nothing to lose, I decided to learn about them and see if they could help me. It was from that point that everything began to change in my life. And I'm talking about massive changes. From a position of waiting tables and being virtually penniless to having my first acting role in over a year and a contract worth a quarter of a million dollars."

"You're kidding!" exclaimed the young man. "Your life changed that dramatically?"

Mr. Edgely nodded. "That's the power of the secrets. When I met the old man I was despondent about my acting career. I couldn't seem to get a break. I couldn't even get an agent, let alone a job. Over thirty agents turned me down, some of them even advised me to get another career. They said I just didn't have what it takes. And then I met the old Chinese man and discovered the secrets of Abundant Wealth.

"All of the secrets helped me in one way or another, but the one that, looking back, I think I most needed to learn was the power of persistence."

The young man took out his notepad and pen, ready to write notes.

"Persistence is the most underrated quality in human achievement," continued Mr. Edgely. "Calvin Coolidge, the thirty-fourth president of the United States of America wrote:

Nothing in the world can take the place of persistence. Talent will not; nothing is more common than unsuccessful men with talent. Genius will not; unrewarded genius is almost a proverb. Education alone will not; the world is full of educated derelicts. Persistence and determination alone are omnipotent.

"One of the most important differences between someone who succeeds in anything," explained Mr. Edgely, "whether it is in acquiring wealth or becoming top of their chosen profession, and someone who doesn't, is that the successful people persist, they never quit. Even when faced with obstacles or rejection, they never give up. They know what they want and they continue pursuing their goal until they achieve it.

"In fact, many of the most successful people throughout history have acknowledged that they would not have achieved what they did had they not been persistent.

"Imagine for a moment that you are trying to invent a new product. How many times would you be willing to try before you decide to give up? One hundred? One thousand? Two thousand? Maybe five thousand?"

The young man shrugged his shoulders.

"Because," continued Mr. Edgely, "Thomas Edison, one of the most successful inventors who ever lived, had to make over ten thousand separate attempts before he invented the world's first light bulb. If he hadn't been persistent, we might not have had the light bulb today.

"Or if you were a member of a rock band, how many times would record companies have to turn you down before you decided to give up? Five? Ten? Maybe twenty?"

The young man smiled. "I think I would have got the message by the twentieth time."

"Well, one band didn't. And if they had, they would have missed out on becoming one of the most successful rock bands of all time. Because the Beatles were turned down by over fifty different record companies before they got their first recording contract!

"Let me give you one last example: imagine a young man with dreams of becoming a great statesman. Despite his efforts, by the time he reaches thirty-two he is bankrupt. When he is thirty-five, his childhood sweetheart dies and a year later he suffers a nervous breakdown. In the following years he loses one election after another. When should he give up?"

"I don't know, but that doesn't sound like a man who would ever become a great statesman," said the young man.

Mr. Edgely smiled. "The man I described was, in fact, Abraham Lincoln."

The young man wrote down some notes. "I had no idea that such successful people have failed or were rejected so often," he admitted.

"Of course. In fact, successful people are successful precisely because they have failed so many times."

The young man smiled as he noted it down. Looking up from his notebook he said, "But I don't understand, are you saying that if we keep trying we will eventually succeed?"

"Yes. Most of the time, we will," answered Mr. Edgely, "providing we learn from our mistakes. Thomas Edison didn't do the same experiment ten thousand times to invent the light bulb, he learned from the results of each experiment and made appropriate changes.

"Persistence is a quality we all have as infants," explained Mr. Edgely. "After all, have you ever seen a baby that, despite long hours of struggling and falling down each day, doesn't eventually learn to walk?"

"But why do we lose that quality?" asked the young man.

"Sometimes we become afraid of failure and rejection. Sometimes we lose faith in ourselves. But what we forget is that failure and rejection are important ingredients in success. In fact, you could say the more failure and rejection you experience, the more successful you will become."

"I don't understand," said the young man. "How can that be true?"

"Because failure and rejection are necessary steps on the ladder to success. We learn from our mistakes and move closer to our goals. George Bernard Shaw put it this way. He said: 'When I was a young man I observed that nine out of ten things I did were failures. I didn't want to be a failure so I did ten times more work.'

"You can take any person who is extremely successful in their chosen career," explained Mr. Edgely, "and you will find that invariably they had to go through a series of failures and rejections before they became successful.

"When I first discovered the importance of persistence, I had virtually lost hope of getting an acting job, let alone of becoming a famous actor. But I could see that if I was to be a success, I would have to keep trying. I believed in myself and my abilities. I had a specific goal, I drew up an organized plan of action and I kept applying for jobs until eventually, nine months later, I got one."

"But it's not easy persisting if you are failing and not getting results," said the young man.

"Nobody said it was easy," said Mr. Edgely. "If it was easy everybody would do it. But one of the differences between successful people and unsuccessful people is that as far as successful people are concerned, there are no failures, only learning experiences."

"What do you mean by that?" asked the young man.

"Well, simply this: if you don't get the result you wanted or expected, you learn from the experience and try again. In fact, there is no way to succeed at anything unless you are willing to make mistakes, to learn and to move on.

"Theodore Roosevelt put it this way:

Far better it is, to dare mighty things, to win glorious triumphs even though checkered with failure, than to take ranks with those poor spirits who neither win much nor suffer much, because they live in the great twilight that knows neither victory nor defeat.

"One of the reasons why so few people succeed is that many are not willing to go through the failure and rejection. But there is one thing that will make persistence through times of failure easier."

"What is that?" asked the young man.

"The way you analyze each attempt. What I mean is that when people fail they usually focus on what they did wrong. That in turn makes them feel bad about themselves, they lose confidence and are no longer motivated to try again. Those who succeed focus on what they did that was right. So even if they didn't achieve the desired result, they ask themselves, 'what did I do that was right to last as long as I did?'"

"I'm not with you," said the young man.

"Well, let's take a computer salesman. He picks up the telephone to cold call a prospect. He introduces himself and asks the prospect if he would buy a new computer. The prospect says no. End of conversation. What did he do right to last as long as he did? He had made a call, got through to a next prospect and made a sales pitch. With that knowledge, he tries again, but this time asks a different question. He asks the prospect if he is interested in finding out about the latest computer technology for businesses. This time the prospect says that he is interested but doesn't have the time to look into it. What did the salesman do right? He asked a different question and established that the prospect was too busy to think about buying new computers. The salesman tries again, calling another prospect and this time he asks another different question. 'Would you be interested in sparing five minutes to allow me to show you how you can cut both the cost and time of your office administration by at least fifty percent? This prospect is busy but he is interested to learn how he could cut his costs. It won't cost him anything to spare five minutes at the end of the day so he books an appointment. The salesman has succeeded in making an appointment and has an opportunity to make his sales pitch.

"That is how all great inventors think; they ask, 'what did I do that enabled me to last as long as I did?' and that same question is what we have to ask if we want to be able to persist in any endeavor whether it be selling products or creating wealth."

The young man quickly scribbled down a note as Mr. Edgely continued. "I used to think that our lives were predetermined by fate," said Mr. Edgely. "Either it was written in the stars or it wasn't. But now I am firmly convinced that we all have the power to create our own destinies.

"One of the most inspiring things I ever learned in my life was that who we are is bigger than anything that can ever happen to us. Whatever happens, if we adopt the approach of a stonecutter and keep hammering away, we will succeed."

Mr. Edgely then reached into his pocket and took out a piece of paper. "I have carried this with me every day," he said, handing it to the young man, "as a reminder of the power of persistence."

The young man opened it up and found a short poem:

Don't Quit!
When things go wrong, as they sometimes will,
When the road you are trudging seems all uphill,
When the funds are low and the debts are high,
And you want to smile but have to sigh,
When care is pressing you down a bit,
Rest if you must—but don't you quit!

Life is queer with its twists and turns,
As every one of us sometimes learns,
And many a failure turns about
When he might have won if he had stuck it out;
Don't give up, though the pace seems slow—
You might succeed with another blow . . .

Success is failure turned inside out—
The silver tint of the clouds of doubt—
And you can never tell how close you are,
It may be near when it seems afar;
So stick to the fight when you are hardest hit—
It's when things get worse that you mustn't quit!

Edgar A. Guest

That night the young man thought long and hard about his life. Looking back over the years he could now see that persistence hadn't been a quality he had nurtured. As soon as things got difficult or he found obstacles in his way, he invariably gave up and looked for something else to try. He realized now after meeting with Mr. Edgely that if he wanted to succeed at anything, he would have to resolve to change and become like the stonecutter. Whatever obstacles may block his path, he would have to persist and never stop persisting, until he succeeded.

He took out his notepad and read over the notes he had made in his meeting with Mr. Edgely one more time:

The sixth secret of Abundant Wealth—the power of persistence.

Success is not usually the result of one effort but rather the accumulation of many efforts.

The difference between people who succeed and those who don't is not necessarily talent, it is persistence!

Always ask yourself after any action that did not produce the desired result: "What did I do that was right to last as long as I did?" That way you will always be encouraged to try again.

If you adopt the approach of a stonecutter and persist, and never stop persisting, and learn from every experience, you will always succeed in your endeavors.

The POWER of CONTROLLED EXPENDITURE

The next person on the young man's list was a woman by the name of Judy Orman. The young man telephoned her the following morning to confirm their appointment that afternoon.

Mrs. Orman ran her own business from an office in her home which was a large, detached house in a sought-after suburb on the edge of the city. She was a large-framed black woman, a little shorter than the young man, and looked to be in her early forties. Mrs. Orman was an attractive woman with deep brown eyes and long braided hair. She was casually dressed in a bright red baggy sweater and black leggings.

Mrs. Orman's office was at the back of the house. It was a bright, spacious room; in the far corner stood a large antique-style oak desk and a matching high-backed executive chair. To the right of the desk was a computer workstation containing a computer, two telephones and an array of state-of-the-art office equipment. To the left of the desk were French windows which opened onto a large york-stoned terrace overlooking a sizable and very attractive garden. The gentle gradient of the lawn sloped down to a magnificent weeping willow tree which stood only a few meters away from a single-story timber outhouse. But what made the view so special was the flowing river onto which the garden backed.

"What a wonderful view," admired the young man. "It must be great to look out upon as you work."

Mrs. Orman smiled. "Thank you. It is. It was always one of my dreams to be able to work from home and look out over a river. And, of course, one of the major benefits of working from home is that I get to spend more quality time with my family instead of having to waste hours every day commuting through traffic or on crowded trains or buses. I know people who travel to and from work for nearly three hours every day. Can you imagine? That's fifteen hours or the equivalent of two working days per week!

"Time is the most precious commodity in the world, far more valuable than gold because, once gone, it can never be replaced."

Mrs. Orman gestured for the young man to sit down in one of the armchairs and she sat in the other one. "So, you want to know about the secrets of Abundant Wealth?" she said.

The young man nodded. "Yes," he answered. "How did you first find out about them?"

"Well, let me see, I first heard about them ten years ago. I was in very different circumstances then than I am today: my first husband and I had recently separated and I was up to my eyeballs in debt; there were thousands owing on my credit cards, and the mortgage company was suing me for non-payment and seeking to repossess my home. The court gave me one month to come to an agreement with my creditors or I would lose everything."

"Good grief!" exclaimed the young man. "How did you get out of that?"

"I remember the day very well," Mrs. Orman continued. "I was in tears, sitting on a bench outside the courtroom, agonizing about what I was going to do. The situation seemed so hopeless. Then I felt the warmth of a hand on my shoulder and turned to find a little old Chinese man sitting next to me. He was dressed in a tailored suit and I assumed he was a court official. He asked me if I needed any help. I thanked him for his concern, but told him there was nothing he could do. He stayed beside me though and talked to me. I don't remember much of what he said, but one particular phrase stayed with me, and that was what he referred to as the golden rule of problem solving: 'When you think you have exhausted all possibilities remember one thing . . . you haven't!'"

The young man smiled to himself as he remembered the old Chinese man giving him the same advice.

"The old man talked about 'secrets of Abundant Wealth.' Of course, I had never heard of them before, but I was intrigued by what the old man had to say. It was the first time I had heard someone suggest that we can control our own destinies. All my life I had been told that life can be kind or cruel, we would win or we would lose . . . it was all down to fate or luck. And here was an old man telling me that we are all in control of our own destinies, and that we all have the power to create wealth in our lives.

"Before the old man left, he gave me a piece of paper which he said would help me solve my problems. I was completely perplexed when I looked at it because all it contained was a list of ten names and telephone numbers."

"I know the feeling," said the young man, smiling.

"I have to say that I didn't hold out much hope," continued Mrs. Orman, "but I contacted all of the people on the old man's list and listened to what they had to say.

They all had fascinating testimonies, and although I wasn't convinced that the secrets of Abundant Wealth would work for me, I tried to apply what I learned and gradually my life started to change."

The young man took out his trusted notepad and pen and began to scribble down some notes. When he finished writing he looked up at Mrs. Orman. "How exactly did your life change?" he asked.

"First of all, I was happier because I felt more in control of my life. But, to my amazement, within three years I had cleared all of my debts *and* saved enough money to start up my own small business."

"And which of the secrets do you think was most responsible for that change?" asked the young man who was intrigued by Mrs. Orman's experience.

"They all helped me," answered Mrs. Orman, "but looking back, the one secret that had the most profound effect on my life at that time was the power of controlled expenditure."

"Controlled expenditure?" repeated the young man. "Do you mean budgeting?"

"Sort of, yes," replied Mrs. Orman.

"How can budgeting help you to create wealth?" asked the young man.

"First of all, remember that wealth is not determined by how much money you earn, but by how well you can live on the money you earn," answered Mrs. Orman.

"What's the difference?" said the young man. "Surely, the more money you earn, the more things you can afford and the better lifestyle you can lead."

"That doesn't necessarily follow," answered Mrs. Orman solemnly. "In fact, you'll find that very often the more money you earn, the more money you will spend and the more sacrifices you may have to make. For example a bigger salary may involve longer hours at work and therefore less time with your family. If you earn a large salary but are unable to spend more than a few hours a week with your children, could you consider yourself wealthy?"

The young man rubbed his chin. "I see what you mean," he said.

"Wealth has more to do with the quality of your life than with the amount of money you make," explained Mrs. Orman. "You don't have to be a multimillionaire to experience Abundant Wealth, all you need is to have sufficient means to live your life the way you want to live it!

"Therefore, if you want to be wealthy," continued Mrs. Orman, "one of the first things you need to learn is how to live within your means, and that means controlling your expenditure. One thousand dollars income and nine hundred dollars expenditure leads to contentment, but one thousand dollars income and eleven hundred dollars expenditure leads to misery," she said. "If your expenses are greater than your income, you're heading for trouble."

"I understand what you're saying," said the young man. "Living within a budget may help prevent the accumulation of debts, but it can't help you to increase your income, can it?"

"Oh, but it can, and it does! Controlling your expenditure is not only necessary if you are to live happily within your income," insisted Mrs. Orman. "It is a vital part of creating more income."

"Really?" said the young man. "In what way?"

"Nobody can create wealth and maintain it without a steady stream of accumulating income, you agree?" The young man nodded. "However much capital you may have," continued Mrs. Orman, "it will, of course, eventually be depleted if you spend it and don't have any income to replenish it.

"The only way you can create a steady stream of income is by either earning more money or making some of the money that you earn work for you."

"You mean saving or investing money?" asked the young man.

"Yes. If you save regularly and invest wisely, your money will earn interest and grow."

"But, first you've got to have enough money to save and invest," argued the young man. "I mean, with the bills I have, I can barely get by let alone save anything."

"Believe me, it can be done," assured Mrs. Orman, "but of course you have to be committed. You have to start by saying, 'Part of my income is mine to keep.'"

"But all of my income is mine to keep," said the young man.

"Well, you just said that you barely have enough to get by, so at the moment, none of it is really yours. Your income is mostly going to pay bills."

"Well . . . yes . . . but . . . " stumbled the young man.

"Many people—and I was one of them—struggle to make ends meet and feel as if they are working just to pay their bills," continued Mrs. Orman. "But that's often because they don't give themselves any of their income.

"If you want to start to create Abundant Wealth in your life you need to start to pay yourself a proportion of your income, and to use that proportion to save and invest to create a flow of income."

"I don't think I can afford to save much, if anything," persisted the young man.

"Then you have not controlled your expenditure wisely," replied Mrs. Orman. "Believe me, you can't afford not to save and invest."

"Maybe so, but it's easier said than done."

"Well, all I can tell you is what I found worked for me. Start by putting aside ten percent of your income.

Whatever you earn, control your living expenses to within nine tenths of your net income. I promise you that it's easier than you think. You have to be disciplined about it, and make it a habit. It might mean having to give up a few of life's luxuries in the short term, but in the long run it will be worth it.

"Let me show you something," Mrs. Orman said. "Let's take a hypothetical situation, and say that you managed to save more or less $30 a week, that's $1,500 a year, and you invested that money in a savings scheme that gave you an annual return of eight percent. After twenty-five years you would have paid in $37,500, but the interest would have accumulated your savings to $118,425!"

"Really!" exclaimed the young man. "How is that possible?"

"Compound interest!" replied Mrs. Orman. "The first year your interest is eight percent of $1,500, but the second year your interest is eight percent of $3,120. You are, in effect, receiving interest on your original interest. And it is remarkable how quickly savings can accumulate when interest is compounded. For example, if you saved $1,500 a year for thirty-five years and got an annual eight percent return, you would have paid in $52,000, but accumulated over $279,000!"

"But what about inflation?" asked the young man. "If prices rise by eight percent and your investment only earns eight percent, you're no better off than when you started."

"That's a fair point," answered Mrs. Orman. "And you are perfectly correct—the real rate of growth of your savings is the rate that it grows over and above the rate of inflation. I only chose eight percent as an example to illustrate how you can make your money grow by controlling your expenditure and saving regularly.

"Of course, when saving and investing, you need to have specialized knowledge or to consult someone who has specialized knowledge about investments, like a financial consultant or accountant. You need to ensure that you select the savings schemes and investments which are best suited to your needs. This will depend upon your income, your marital status, tax incentives and whether you are able and willing to forgo being able to access your money for a certain period of time.

"But the important point is the principle of controlling your expenditure, setting aside money to save and invest, so that you can make your money work for you to produce income for the future. And, although it may sound obvious, the sooner you start controlling your expenditure, the better off you will be. Even a delay of ten years can make a huge difference. That's why it is so important to start saving in your youth."

"Surely, it wouldn't make so much difference if someone started saving in their thirties rather than their twenties?" said the young man.

"Well, you judge for yourself," answered Mrs. Orman. "Who would be better off on their sixty-fifth birthday; a man who began saving $1,500 a year when he was 29 years old and continued saving $1,500 every year until he was sixty-five, or a man who began saving $1,500 a year when he was 19 years old but stopped saving when he was 29? Assuming that they saved their money in the same investment which gave an annual return of eight percent, who would have more on their sixty-fifth birthday?"

"Surely, the man who began saving when he was 29. Although he started later, he continued investing for thirty-six years and paid in nearly four times more than the other man," answered the young man.

Mrs. Orman gave a mischievous grin. "In actual fact your man would have paid in $54,000 and this would have grown to $303,105 by his sixty-fifth birthday. But in the case of the man who began saving when he was 19 years old, despite the fact that he only saved for ten years and therefore only paid in $15,000, his account has accumulated to $374,852.35!

"Are you serious?" exclaimed the young man. "Ten years makes that much of a difference?"

"The figures speak for themselves, don't they?" replied Mrs. Orman.

The young man took a deep breath, realizing that he would have to start saving soon. But he still wasn't sure how he would be able to put money aside.

"I admit controlling your expenditure and saving regularly sounds good in theory," he said, "but how easy is it to do in practice? How did you manage to do it?"

"When I first heard about the importance of controlling my expenditure, I had my reservations as well, especially as I had a number of creditors to whom I owed a lot of money. But I knew that if it was going to work I would have to try and set aside ten percent of my income to invest for the future as well as pay off my debts."

"How can you save and pay off your debts at the same time?" asked the young man.

"I approached each of my creditors and explained my financial difficulties. I then offered to pay them in monthly installments from my income. They could see that I didn't have the means to pay them all at once and at least by paying in installments, they would all get their money back eventually.

"I then made a budget. I would live on seventy percent of my income, use twenty percent to pay off my debts and ten percent I would set aside for myself. That way, I felt good about the fact that I was clearing my debts and happy that I was also able to start to create some wealth for myself. Of course, it was by no means easy. I had to cut out certain luxuries—for instance, I took homemade sandwiches to work instead of buying lunches, I bought fewer pre-packed meals, I had fewer nights out and I only bought clothes in the sales. But, once I made that budget, I found that I was more motivated at work and within a few years, not only had I cleared all of my debts but I had also accumulated enough savings to start my own small business. In fact, it was having to control my expenditure that inspired my business."

"In what way?" asked the young man.

"Well, as you can imagine, I had to live within a fairly tight budget and I found that I could usually get bargains at auctions. Then, one day, when showing off one of my bargain purchases to a friend, an idea came to me. My friend asked me how she could find out when other auctions were taking place and it suddenly occurred to me that there would probably be lots of people who would be interested in attending auctions all over the county.

"I set up a monthly newsletter giving details of the auctions throughout the county. I put a small advert in local newspapers and charged a modest fee for an annual subscription, and the response was incredible!

"Then I reasoned that the service could be extended to the whole of the country. And so I placed adverts in other counties and pretty soon I was getting subscriptions to my newsletters by the sack load."

"That's fantastic!" said the young man.

"Yes. It is, isn't it? And it was all thanks to the power of controlled expenditure. I wouldn't have been able to save enough money to start my own business if I hadn't controlled my expenses, and my business wouldn't have succeeded if I hadn't controlled my operating expenses. Did you know that over eighty percent of new businesses fail in the first twelve months of trading because they over-capitalize and spend beyond their means?"

The young man shook his head.

"But, more importantly," continued Mrs. Orman, "controlling my expenditure ensured that, apart from my business, I was able to build wealth for the future by making my money work for me."

"You really think it's that important?" asked the young man.

"Absolutely," assured Mrs. Orman. "Now I'm not, for one moment, saying that you should live like a monk and deny yourself all of life's luxuries in the pursuit of long-term wealth. But if wealth is important to you, then some luxuries may have to be sacrificed. It means that you should only spend within your means, and never borrow or accumulate debts that you can't repay.

"One man I met who was a house decorator on a low income, living in very basic rented accommodation with a wife and four children to support, took out a $9,000 loan for his business, but spent it on a six-week holiday for himself and his family in Disneyworld, Florida. When he got back from the holiday he couldn't even afford to buy his children new shoes. His family will never be well provided for and he will almost certainly end up living off state benefits in old age all because he hasn't learned the importance of controlled expenditure.

"You see, many people mistakenly believe that their lives are controlled by fate or luck or circumstances. The truth is, of course, that we have no one to blame for the situations in which we find ourselves, but us. We struggle to make a living when instead we could be designing a life.

"This was the most important lesson I think I have ever learned. Your destiny is not written in the stars as some people would have you believe; your destiny is written by you, and you alone, each and every day of your life. People all too often blame the state of the economy, the government, their parents and even the weather for their problems. But the truth is, the only person responsible for your life is you, and only you have the power to change it. Our thoughts and our actions determine the course we take in life and the secrets of Abundant Wealth show you how to take a more profitable course and create the destiny of your dreams."

The young man, who had been taking notes as Mrs. Orman spoke, finished writing and looked up. "So what you're saying is that controlling your expenditure won't bring you riches overnight, but it will build Abundant Wealth for the future?"

"Precisely," said Mrs. Orman. "And virtually anyone can take advantage of it. Firstly, it ensures that you don't get into unnecessary debt. Secondly, it enables you to make your money work for you."

"But you've got to wait a long time to reap the benefits," said the young man. "I accept that controlling your expenditure and putting savings aside can help you in old age, but how can it help you create wealth now or in the immediate future?"

"If you want wealth in abundance, you have to build it, and it needs firm foundations. Controlling your expenditure won't make you rich overnight, or over a year for that matter, but it will enable you to build for the future. It enables you to better take care of your family, it keeps you out of debt and, at the very least, it ensures that you will be one of less than ten percent of people who are financially independent in their old age. By putting aside just ten percent of your income each week, you will slowly but surely accumulate capital that can be invested to create wealth.

"But always beware of 'get-rich-quick' schemes," warned Mrs. Orman. "Highly speculative investments can be dangerous. It is better to have a little caution than a big regret! There are times when you have got to take risks in life, it's true, but calculated risks—not random gambling."

The young man finished scribbling and looked up from his notepad.

"But once you have accumulated a lot of money," he said, "surely you don't need to control your expenditure."

"You will find that a person's expenses invariably increase in direct proportion to their income," replied Mrs. Orman. "They immediately spend more on a bigger house, a better car, organize more expensive holidays, buy designer clothes and go to expensive restaurants—unless they make a conscious decision to control their expenditure. It's true that there are a few individuals who don't need to worry about how much they spend, but most people do. Even many millionaires. In fact, one of the reasons why most people who win the lottery end up penniless is because they don't control their expenditure. They spend, and spend with no thought of the future. Remember that wealth is about creating a continual flow of income. If you don't produce a flow of income, eventually your money will dry up, like a lake that has no river to feed it. And that is why you cannot create Abundant Wealth or maintain it without using the power of controlled expenditure."

Later that day the young man read over the notes he had made during his meeting with Mrs. Orman:

The seventh secret of Abundant Wealth—the power of controlled expenditure.

Wealth is not determined by how much money you earn, but by how well you can live on the money you earn.

Controlling your expenditure helps you live happily within your existing income and helps to create more income.

Anybody who has limited resources needs to control their expenditure to ensure a continual flow of income.

Part of your income is yours to keep. Set aside ten percent of your income to invest. This will then begin to build wealth for your future.

Let your money work for you rather than you always working for money.

The POWER of INTEGRITY

There was hardly a person in the city who hadn't heard of Honest Henry's. It was a chain of stores renowned for selling quality household products at unbeatable prices. The ethos was simple; if you wanted a reliable product but were not concerned about brand-named products, then you couldn't do better than Honest Henry's. There were no gimmicks or tricks; product packaging was kept simple and inexpensive, and the stores offered a no-quibble money-back guarantee on all sales. The founder and owner of the chain was Henry Brookes; he was also the eighth person on the young man's list.

When the young man entered his office, Mr. Brookes immediately rose from his chair and greeted the young man with a warm handshake. Mr. Brookes was a small, rotund man, 54 years of age who wore thick-rimmed, black spectacles which made his eyes appear like tiny marbles in his large, round face.

The young man briefly told Mr. Brookes about his meeting with the old Chinese man.

"Fantastic!" exclaimed Mr. Brookes. "So you want to be wealthy?"

"Yes," admitted the young man.

"And what do you think of the secrets of Abundant Wealth so far?"

"They're certainly interesting," replied the young man. "What do you know about them?"

"Let me take you back some thirty years," said Mr. Brookes. "I was in my early twenties and desperately wanted to make money, a lot of money. I didn't care how I did it, my goal was to become a millionaire by my fortieth birthday. And that was my biggest problem."

"Why?" asked the young man. "I thought that definiteness of purpose is essential to create Abundant Wealth?"

"It is," replied Mr. Brookes. "But I'm not talking about my goal to become a millionaire—that was fine— my problem was that I didn't care how I did it. I had been so concerned with the dream of becoming a millionaire that I neglected one of the most important secrets of Abundant Wealth . . . the power of integrity.

"You know the Bible asks, 'what does it profit a man if he gains the whole world, but loses his soul?' And I promise you that no truer words were ever written. There are no poorer people than those who have no integrity or self-respect. It doesn't matter how much money you have, you will never feel wealthy, and any wealth that you do accumulate will be temporary if you have no integrity. Trying to build wealth by deceptive and fraudulent means is like trying to build a house on sand. It won't last.

"I remember one of my first jobs was working for a double-glazing company. It was a complete scam really; we would knock on people's doors and offer a free inspection of their existing windows. Naturally we would recommend new ones and then tell them that we could replace their windows for half the normal price if we could use their house in our promotional materials.

The average job would cost $9,000 and we would tell them that they could therefore make a savings of $4,500 if we could photograph their house before and after the windows were installed.

"It was easy too," explained Mr. Brookes. "I found that I had a talent for persuading people to sign on the dotted line. I would get twenty percent commission of the cost to the customer plus bonuses, and as you can imagine, I did very well. I could earn over $3,000 in one week.

"But one day everything changed; I knocked on a door and an old Chinese man answered. He invited me in and I went through all of my sales patter. When I finished, he said, 'Who will profit if I buy new windows, me or you?' 'Hopefully, we both will,' I said. Then he looked me squarely in the eye and said, 'Do you really believe that I need your windows? In your professional opinion, are the existing ones really unsuitable for their purpose?'

"There was something about the old man, I'm not sure what, but whatever it was, it made me feel uncomfortable. I couldn't lie to him, and for the first time since I took up the job, I gave an honest answer. I stood up to leave. The old man rose from his chair and, grasping my hand, thanked me for being honest. He said he could see I was eager to do well in life and asked me if I wanted to know a better way of making a living.

"Naturally I was curious, so I stayed and listened to what he had to say. I thought he might know of a fantastic money-making scheme, but as it turned out, he told me about the secrets of Abundant Wealth. He gave me a list of people who, he said, would be able to explain the secrets to me in more detail and so I contacted and met all of them to try and find out more about the secrets.

"Those secrets changed my entire attitude toward life and, as a result, my life changed. Not least of which was my income which within the next two years had quadrupled."

"How did you do it?" asked the young man.

"I started off selling a variety of household products from a market stall. Within two years I had my own shop. Three years later I had a chain of thirty shops and two years later the total had reached seventy-five with a multimillion dollar annual turnover."

"And you credit your success to the secrets of Abundant Wealth?" asked the young man.

"No doubt about it," said Mr. Brookes. "And the secret that I think had the biggest impact on my life was the power of integrity."

"Integrity?" quizzed the young man.

"Yes. A principled, honest approach to business."

"Really?" said the young man. "Being honest helped you to succeed?"

"Of course. Honesty and integrity are essential if you want to succeed and create Abundant Wealth in your life and I'll tell you why. First, it is difficult for anyone with a modicum of a conscience to feel good about themselves if they are dishonest in their business dealings. If you don't feel good about yourself and what you do, it's difficult to keep motivated.

"Secondly, whatever we do in life comes back to us. You know the saying, 'What goes around, comes around'?"

"Of course."

"Well, it's true. It's a basic law in Life and all religious scriptures warn of this law; the Hindu religion calls it Karma, the Bible calls it judgment—you reap what you sow—whatever you choose to call it, it is a law that none of us can escape. Our deeds, our words and even our thoughts are like boomerangs, they always return to us."

"So you're saying that if you deceive people, you will be deceived," said the young man.

"Exactly. It might not be by the same person you deceived, but it will always come back to you."

The young man thought about his own job. There were times when he did things which weren't strictly honest—the most obvious one that came to mind was deceiving his employer by taking off sick days when he wasn't really sick. He knew it wasn't the right thing to do, but had reasoned that everyone else did it. Why should he be the only one who didn't?

"What do you do," he said, "if everybody else is doing something dishonest?"

"What other people do," answered Mr. Brookes, "is their own business. They can't escape the law of Karma either, so it is foolish to use other people's actions to justify your own behavior.

"Furthermore," continued Mr. Brookes, "all deception and fraud will eventually come to light. It always catches up with us in the end. And when it does, whatever you have built will fall down upon you like a ton of bricks."

"But let's face it," said the young man, "most rich people are crooked in some way, aren't they?"

"Not at all. The notion that all rich people are crooks is as ridiculous as suggesting that all poor people are saints. In fact, wherever you see poverty or lack, you will invariably also see crime. The highest crime rates are found in the poorest areas."

"Why is that?" asked the young man.

"Because poverty and lack are often used as excuses for crime. Abundant Wealth can only be created honestly and with integrity."

"But, in my experience, most people in business are lying or cheating."

"It sounds like you are doing business with the wrong people," said Mr. Brookes.

"But where do you draw the line between what is

right or wrong, especially if your competitors are all dishonest?" asked the young man.

"The easiest thing to do is ask yourself a series of questions when considering any course of action. The first question is, 'Is it legal?' If it is an illegal activity then you are automatically heading for trouble.

"The next question is, 'Is it moral?'"

"Why should you worry about that?" asked the young man. "If it isn't illegal, you can't get into any real trouble."

"That's true as far as the police are concerned," answered Mr. Brookes. "But remember, what goes around, comes around. If you are earning your living by immoral means, it will come to light eventually, and then, how will you feel when everybody discovers what you have been doing? You only have to open a newspaper to see how immoral acts either in business or personal life can leave a person ruined."

The young man nodded his head in agreement. "Which leads on to the third question, 'Will it make me feel proud of myself?' If you have no pride in what you are doing, you are doing the wrong thing.

"The fourth question is: 'Would I be happy for my family to know about it?' Would your mother be proud of you if she found out about it? If you were thinking of doing something that would be a source of embarrassment to your family rather than a source of pride, it would be a pretty good indication that it wouldn't be the right thing to do.

"And, the final question is, 'Will I respect myself for having done it?' If you are about to do something that will compromise your principles, you will be sacrificing your self-respect. It is very difficult to live with anyone who you don't respect . . . especially if that person is yourself.

"The ultimate guideline is simply not to do or say anything that you wouldn't want somebody else to say or do to you."

When the young man had finished writing down the questions in his notepad, he looked up at Mr. Brookes. "So you're saying that if any of the answers to these questions are negative, no matter how profitable the business may be, you shouldn't proceed with it?"

"That's it. Too often people make the mistake of trying to make money and acquire wealth without regard for their principles or for basic notions of what is morally right or wrong. They think that money is the end goal; but it isn't, it is the means to obtain *other* goals. And often, if we focused on those other goals rather than money alone, we would find that we would achieve them far more easily."

"Thank you for sharing this with me," said the young man as he got up to leave. "You've certainly given me a lot to think about. I have one final question before I leave; does the old Chinese man still live at the same address?"

"I'm not sure that he ever lived there," said Mr. Brookes.

"What do you mean?"

"Months later, I went back to the house where I met the old man. I just wanted to thank him for his help and tell him how he had helped change my life. But this time there was an elderly couple living there who claimed that they had been living in that house for twenty years. They had never heard of an old Chinese man. I asked the neighbors as well, but nobody had ever heard of him."

That night before going to bed, the young man read over the notes he had made:

The eighth secret of Abundant Wealth—the power of integrity.

"What shall it profit a man if he gains the whole world, but loses his soul?"

Our deeds, our words and even our thoughts are like boomerangs—they always come back to us.

Trying to build wealth by deceptive and fraudulent means is like trying to build a house on sand—it won't last.

When considering any course of action in your business or personal life consider:

Is it legal?

Is it moral?

Will it make me feel proud of myself?

Would I be happy for my family to know about it?

Will I respect myself for having done it?

The POWER of FAITH

The following day the young man woke earlier than usual. His mind was troubled; he knew that the secrets of Abundant Wealth had worked for the people he had met, but would they work for him? That was the question. And the answer was that he just couldn't be sure. He had ideas for his own business, but what if he failed? What if he ended up with less than he already had? He had struggled with the problem through the night, but had awoken no wiser. He had never been good at making important decisions. The wrong choice could be disastrous and would affect the rest of his life. He hoped that the next person on his list might be able to help him in some way.

Despite being bald and in his mid-sixties Simon Lewis retained a youthful vigor about him. He exercised regularly and enjoyed outdoor pursuits which he claimed helped keep him feeling young. He looked every inch a successful businessman dressed in an immaculately pressed, dark gray designer suit with a red paisley tie and matching handkerchief.

Mr. Lewis ran his own life insurance agency from a large complex which he owned on the outskirts of the city. His company was renowned throughout the industry as the market leader in its field with an annual gross turnover which was, at the very least, ten times more than his nearest competitor. Yet, as the young man was to discover, Mr. Lewis hadn't always been the successful, wealthy businessman sitting opposite him. In fact, virtually all of his life—until his sixtieth birthday to be precise—he had struggled financially. Only five years ago he had been living in a cramped, one-bedroomed apartment in one of the less salubrious suburbs and, unable to afford proper office space, had had to make do by running his business from the kitchen on the fourth floor of an old run-down office block.

But here he was today, sitting in front of the young man, founder of one of the most successful life insurance companies in the country. The young man was eager to find out what had turned his fortunes around in such a relatively short space of time.

"It all began a little over five years ago," explained Mr. Lewis. "I was sitting in the kitchen that I was using as my office wondering what I could do to improve my situation. I was approaching my sixtieth birthday and I was in debt with no savings at a time in my life when I ought to have been looking forward to a comfortable retirement. I was reading an article in *Time* magazine that reported that less than eight percent of men and less than two percent of women who reach the age of 65 are financially independent. Less than one percent are what you and I would describe as affluent or wealthy. It was a depressing thought, my situation seemed so hopeless and I sat there and put my hands together and prayed that something would happen to help me out of my situation.

"Suddenly a voice said, 'Don't worry, it may never happen!' I looked up and found an old Oriental man in the room smiling at me. He asked me why I was working from a kitchen. I explained that times were tough, and he nodded. 'Tough times never last,' he said, 'but tough people do!'

"We started talking and it wasn't long before the old man mentioned the secrets of Abundant Wealth. I had never heard of them before, but everything that the old man said made sense. Before he left the room, he handed me a list of ten names and telephone numbers and said that if I wanted to change my life and begin to create Abundant Wealth, I should contact those people.

"Needless to say, I contacted all of the people on the old man's list and it was as if a miracle happened—my life did change, more dramatically than I would have believed at the time. And it was all thanks to the secrets of Abundant Wealth."

"In what way did they help you?" asked the young man.

"They showed me that I was responsible for my position in life and I had the power to change it. But I think the one secret that was particularly helpful to me at a time when I was beginning to lose hope and confidence in the future was the power of faith."

"Faith?" repeated the young man. "What has faith to do with wealth?"

"Everything," replied Mr. Lewis. "Everything in Life begins with faith. We wouldn't pursue a dream, we wouldn't start up a business, we wouldn't invest in, or save for, the future unless we first had faith that what we were attempting to do would work out. Once we allow doubts to overtake us, all too often we stop trying and give up.

"At the time when I met the old Chinese man I had been trying to think of ways to improve my business. The only idea that I had was a particular advertising campaign in a national financial newspaper. The only problem was that it was risky because it was expensive and there was no guarantee that it would work. But, if it did work, the returns would be high."

"What did you do?" asked the young man.

"Nothing," replied Mr. Lewis. "I kept thinking 'what if it doesn't work?' It would have totally ruined me. I would have had to take out a large bank loan to finance the advertising campaign so if it didn't work out, I would be paying that loan off for the next five years!

"And what reason did I have to think it would succeed? I had never been very successful in the past, so how could I be sure I could succeed now?

"And then one of the people I met who was on the old man's list said to me that there is really only one question to ask yourself at times of hesitation and doubt and that is: 'What would you do if you knew you couldn't fail?' And I knew, of course, that if I was certain that I couldn't fail, I would take out the loan and initiate the advertising campaign. So the man said: 'There is your answer. Do whatever it is you would do if you knew you couldn't fail.' Then he wrote something down on a piece of paper and handed it to me. He had written a single sentence, but it left a deep and lasting impression on me. That sentence was: 'Be bold, and mighty forces will come to your aid!'

"Be bold! I had never been bold before. I had tended to let fears and doubts prevent me from taking action in the past. In fact, with the benefit of hindsight, I think that was one of the reasons why I had never been able to do well in business before. I had always let my doubts and fears stop me from taking decisive action when it mattered."

The young man could empathize with what Mr. Lewis was saying. He knew he had a tendency to procrastinate when faced with important decisions—a trait which wasn't conducive to succeeding in business, but what could he do about it?

"You know," continued Mr. Lewis, "throughout my life I often heard people say that it is better to try and fail than not to have tried at all. But, in my experience, I think many people really believe, deep down in their hearts, that it is better not to try and then wish that if they had tried they would have succeeded, than to try and fail.

"Most people are afraid of failure, of messing up, but the truth is that the only way you can really fail is by not trying.

"Providing you try something, you can never fail totally because at the very least, you will have learned something from the experience.

"Too many people stop themselves from creating wealth by being afraid of failure and so they never take risks. But life is a risk. Let me show you something," Mr. Lewis said, handing the young man a framed piece of poetry to read:

Risks
To laugh is to risk appearing the fool.
To weep is to risk appearing sentimental.
To reach out for another is to risk involvement.
To expose your feelings is to risk exposing your
    true self.
To place your ideas, your dreams before a crowd is
    to risk their loss.
To love is to risk not being loved in return.
To live is to risk dying.
To hope is to risk despair.
But risks must be taken, because the greatest
    hazard in life is to risk nothing.
The person who risks nothing, does nothing, has
    nothing, and is nothing.
They may avoid suffering and sorrow, but they
    cannot learn, feel, change, grow, love, live.

Chained by their attitudes, they are a slave, they
   have forfeited their freedom.
Only the person who risks is free.

Anon.

"And to take a risk, you have to have faith?" asked
the young man.

"Exactly," said Mr. Lewis. "Now I'm not for one
moment suggesting that you should gamble and take
everything you own and place it on the outcome of the
spin of a roulette wheel. Completely random risk-taking
is foolish and never brings sustained wealth. What I'm
talking about is taking calculated risks relating to projects
you believe in. To follow your goals through an organized plan of action without thought of failure or defeat.

"Your life will change only when you make changes
and you have got to have faith in your power to make
those changes. All change involves an element of uncer-
tainty and therefore risk, but you can't get to second
base unless you have the courage to leave first."

"Yes, but how can you be sure that you make the
right decisions?" asked the young man.

"If in doubt, follow your gut feelings and trust your
intuition—even if it seems illogical or irrational. Your
gut feeling is, more often than not, the one that will lead
you to your dreams. And this is why faith is so important. Once you have faith and you apply it in your life,
you will start to see miracles happen.

"But how can you get faith?" asked the young man. "I
never really had a religious upbringing to speak of, I
wouldn't know where to start."

"You don't need a particular religion to have faith. So
long as you have an open heart, whatever you ask for,
will be given to you regardless of what religious denom-
ination you do or don't belong to. Faith can be learned

and it can be created. One of the best pieces of advice I was ever given concerning faith was to always remember to 'act as if!' Act as if you will succeed, act as if you are capable of achieving your goals, act as if whatever you do it will turn out all right. Act as if you can't fail in your endeavors and that nothing can stop you obtaining your purpose in Life."

"Act as if," repeated the young man as he jotted down notes.

"Only then will you begin to experience success and realize your goals, and you will see that things generally do turn out all right. And once you start achieving things, so your faith in yourself and in Life will increase.

"You can also repeat autosuggestions to yourself to create faith because autosuggestions affect our subconscious beliefs. Anything repeated often enough will become part of your subconscious. So, for instance, some of the autosuggestions I used were: 'God's wealth flows into my life fulfilling my every need and desire,' 'Nothing can stop and nothing can delay the manifestation of Abundant Wealth in my life,' 'Everything that happens, happens for a purpose and a reason and enriches my life,' and 'Anything I ask of Life, I receive at the right time and in the right place.'

"I would repeat these autosuggestions every day. I even wrote them and others down on a small card on the back of my written goals and carried them in my wallet so I could regularly refer to them throughout the day.

"I can't stress enough that one of the most important lessons I have ever learned in my life is that if you have faith, you can achieve anything. Absolutely anything."

"Thank you for sharing this with me," said the young man as he was leaving. "You have really helped me clear things in my own mind."

"I'm pleased to be able to help," answered Mr. Lewis.

"Here," he said, handing the young man a small card. "You might find this helpful."

On the back of the card was a verse:

"Come to the edge" he said.
They said, "We are afraid."
"Come to the edge" he said.
They came.
He pushed them . . .
And they flew.

Guillaume Apollinaire

Later that evening the young man read over the notes he had made of his meeting with Mr. Lewis:

The ninth secret of Abundant Wealth—the power of faith.

When considering any project that you believe in, after you have drawn up an organized plan of action to ensure that it is viable, ask yourself: "What would I do if I knew I couldn't fail?"

Be bold, and mighty forces will come to your aid!

Always "act as if" you will succeed.

Trust your gut feeling—follow your intuition.

Repeat autosuggestions to create faith in yourself. Anything repeated often enough will become part of your subconscious.

He read them through one more time before putting his notepad down and walking over to the window. He knew now what he must do. He must be bold, he must have faith and he must take action.

The
POWER
of
CHARITY

The young man was now becoming excited by what he had learned of the secrets of Abundant Wealth. For the first time in his life, he felt that it really was possible for him to create wealth. Every day he had religiously repeated positive autosuggestions to himself to create subconscious beliefs that would enable him to attract wealth and feel good about it. He had thought long and hard about what he wanted from life—financially, socially, professionally and emotionally—and had written down his goals and began to practice creative visualizations so that he could see himself in his mind achieving those goals.

His biggest dream was to become a writer. But he didn't want to write just any books, he wanted to write books that would make a difference to people who read them. Of course, he had other dreams, dreams of owning a large detached house on its own grounds like the ones he used to pass on his way to the park each morning, and dreams of having sufficient wealth to comfortably provide for a family of his own.

He had then written down a detailed plan of action of the things he could do to help achieve those goals. He had made a budget to control his expenditure; he contacted all of his creditors and informed them of his financial situation. Although he could not afford to pay them all back immediately, he proposed paying them monthly installments. Twenty percent of his income was set aside each month for the repayment of those debts. The arrangement was accepted by his creditors who were pleased that the young man had been open and honest with them rather than trying to evade his debts like so many other debtors. He also ensured that ten percent of everything he earned was set aside for investment. It was true that he had to reduce his spending on non-essential items, but it was a small price to pay for the knowledge that he was now clearing his debts and building wealth for his future.

He understood now that if he was to create Abundant Wealth in his life, he would have to maintain his integrity in all his dealings. He remembered the words of Mr. Brookes, "Life is like a boomerang, whatever you throw out will at some time come back to you."

Realizing now that whatever he did required specialized knowledge, he had enrolled in creative writing classes at night school as well as classes on business management. And now, after meeting and talking with most of the people on the old man's list, he finally had faith that if the secrets of Abundant Wealth could work for them, they could work for him as well. He knew that whatever he conceived and believed, he would eventually achieve.

There was now only one person left on his list, and the young man was naturally very excited to meet him, not least because he was curious to find out what the final secret of Abundant Wealth would be.

Geoffrey Lever lived in a double-fronted four-story mansion in the most affluent part of the city. All of the properties along the large tree-lined streets were impressive mansions renowned for the diplomats, millionaires and celebrities who inhabited them. The young man had visited some beautiful properties during the past weeks, but Mr. Lever's residence surpassed them all. It was an imposing, white eighteenth-century town house.

The interior looked like it had come straight out of the pages of *Home and Garden*, beautifully created by a professional interior decorator with designer fabrics and antique furniture.

A butler greeted the young man at the front door and led him into the drawing room. Three of the four walls were covered from floor to ceiling with books and on the remaining wall there was a large marble fireplace in which a log fire burned and crackled. Above the fireplace was one of the most haunting but beautiful oil paintings the young man had ever seen: two hands with crippled fingers, together as if in prayer reaching upward to the sky.

At that moment the door opened and an elderly man with pure white hair and clear blue eyes entered. The two men shook hands and introduced themselves before sitting in the armchairs in front of the fireplace.

"I saw you were admiring this painting," said Mr. Lever, gesturing to the painting above the fireplace.

"Yes, I was," said the young man. "I don't know much about art, but there's something about this painting. . . "

"There is a beautiful story behind it," said Mr. Lever. "A true story dating back five hundred years to a small village near Nuremberg in Germany. There was a family with eighteen children. The father, a man called Albrecht Dürer, was a goldsmith by trade and worked up to eighteen hours a day just to be able to afford to feed and clothe all of his children. Two of the children displayed a talent for art and they both shared a dream to become artists, but they knew that their father was not financially able to send both of them to the Academy of Arts in Nuremberg. So the two boys made a pact; they would toss a coin. The one who lost would work in the local mines and, with his earnings, pay for the other brother to study at the Academy. Then, after the four years it would take for the one brother to graduate from the Academy, the two brothers would switch roles and the one who had graduated would pay— either from sales of his artwork or, if necessary, from working in the mines—for the other brother to attend the Academy.

"A coin was tossed and Albrecht Dürer the younger won and went off to the Academy while his brother Albert went to work in the mines. Albrecht's talent was quickly recognized and by the time he graduated, four years later, he was able to command considerable fees for his work. He returned to his home village, and after a celebration meal, he rose to toast his beloved brother, Albert, without whose sacrifice Albrecht's success would not have been possible. He ended his speech with the words, 'And now, Albert, my beloved brother, now it is your turn. Now you can go to Nuremburg to pursue your dream and I will take care of you.'

"As the entire family acknowledged Albert's sacrifice and toasted his future at the Academy, he began to weep. Tears streamed down his face, 'No . . . no . . . no,' he repeated. The room was silent, and wiping the tears from his eyes he said in a voice barely above a whisper, 'It is too late for me. I cannot go to Nuremberg. Look!' he said holding up his deformed, arthritic hands, hands in which virtually every bone had been broken during his four years working in the mines. 'It is too painful to hold up a glass to return your toast, never mind hold a paint-brush. For me, it is too late.'

"Albrecht Dürer went on to become a famous artist and today his work hangs in many museums and galleries all over the world. But he never forgot that his success was only made possible by his brother's sacrifice. And, as a lasting tribute to his brother, he created this painting. No more love and pain and tears will you find in any other painting. He made sure that every minute detail of his brother's hands, every scar, every sore was faithfully reproduced. His brother's hands mirror the artist's gratitude and guilt, stretching upward to heaven as if in solemn prayer giving thanks . . . and asking for forgiveness.

"I hung this painting here because it reminds me of what I consider to be one of the most important lessons I learned in my life, which is that abundance of anything is rarely achieved without the help of others. If a person refuses to acknowledge that fact, I don't care how much money he has or how many cars or properties he owns, he will never feel Abundantly Wealthy until he learns the tenth and final secret . . . the power of charity."

"Charity?" said the young man quizzically.

"Yes," assured Mr. Lever. "Charity is an essential element of Abundant Wealth. Of course, if you're only interested in accumulating riches for yourself and your family, then you can do that without being charitable. But, if that is the case, you will never experience Abundant Wealth. Remember, wealth is not solely about the amount of money or possessions you acquire, it is more about the quality of your life."

"But what has charity got to do with the quality of your life?" asked the young man.

"Have you ever done something for another person without any ulterior motive? Helped them just because you were able to help? It could have been something simple, like helping someone cross the road or helping a stranger who was lost."

The young man nodded.

"And how did that make you feel?" asked Mr. Lever.

"Didn't you feel good about it, pleased that you were able to make a difference?"

"Yes."

"How would you have felt if instead of helping, you had walked on by, ignoring the other person's situation?"

"I would probably have felt guilty," admitted the young man.

"That's right. So you can see that by practicing charity, you automatically start to feel good about yourself. You feel like you are able to contribute to society. Consequently, in your subconscious you will believe that you are worthy of receiving more."

"It may help you feel good about yourself," said the young man. "But it doesn't help you create wealth in the first place."

"Have you heard of a principle called 'tithing'?" asked Mr. Lever.

"Yes. Isn't that when members of a church give some of their income to the church?"

"Yes, it is. But the principle began in biblical days by people giving away a certain percentage of their earnings (usually ten percent) to those in need. Now this practice wasn't done only by the very rich, but by everyone except the destitute and the needy.

"Theologians have debated the possible reasons for the principle of tithing. Some assume it was like a primitive form of tax, others suggest it was designed to make a more caring society. But what many neglect to consider is that those who follow it experience benefits far in excess of the value of the money given away."

"By feeling good about themselves you mean?" said the young man.

"That, yes, but also because by giving to others we actually receive ourselves. This is because whatever we do comes back to us. It's like the circle of Life or Karma, call it what you will. Whatever you give comes back to you, and it comes back to you multiplied. It may not be from the same person you gave to, but it will come back to you nonetheless.

"Many years ago, I was struggling to make a living. I worked long hours running my own business, but I just couldn't get ahead. Until one day I met . . . "

"An old Chinese man," interrupted the young man.

"Who else?" Mr. Lever smiled. "And it was through the old man that I learned about the secrets of Abundant Wealth and in particular the power of charity. I argued at the time that I couldn't afford to be charitable, to give money away. But the old man insisted that I couldn't afford *not* to be charitable.

"Naturally I was skeptical about this, but I met someone who assured me that it was when he began giving away ten percent of his income that his financial situation started to improve. So I decided to give it a go, and to my amazement, it worked. I felt better about myself, I was more motivated and . . . my income began to increase. I would go so far as to say that it was the power of charity that made the most dramatic impact on my life.

"Today, I have wealth in abundance; I own this house, a villa in Barbados, and a ski lodge in Switzerland. I drive a vintage Rolls Royce, and I have a net worth of over $15 million."

"And you really believe the principle of charity helped you?" asked the young man.

"Absolutely. Of course it was not the only thing. All

of the secrets of Abundant Wealth played a part. But, when I started to share what I had by giving ten percent of my income away, I began to feel wealthy and it wasn't long before I started to increase my income. Opportunities and contracts came flooding in. Now you could say it was all coincidence, but there are many people who have similar stories to tell."

The young man jotted down some notes as Mr. Lever continued.

"Wealth is sort of like fertilizer. Spread it around a little and it helps things grow. Consequently, you will be enriched. But if you leave it all untouched in one heap it will cause an obnoxious stench and form a breeding ground for dangerous germs and bacteria.

"By giving some of your wealth away, sharing with others who need help, money becomes a source of blessing and returns to you multiplied.

"But you have got to be in a position to help others. You've got to be wealthy to start with," persisted the young man.

"A lot of people would agree with you," said Mr. Lever. "But life doesn't work that way. After all, do you think it is any easier for a person who earns $150,000 to give away $15,000 than it is for a person who earns $15,000 to give away $1,500?"

"I suppose not," said the young man, pursing his lips and squinting his eyes, as if in thought.

"If you get into the habit of giving ten percent of your income away to help others, you will find that it impresses on your subconscious a feeling of abundance—of having more than enough—and thereby starts the flow of abundant wealth in your life.

"It all comes back to this painting," said Mr. Lever pointing above the fireplace. "None of us achieve anything alone. It doesn't matter who you are or where you are from, there will always have been others who have helped you attain your success or wealth. That is why it is important to continue that cycle of charity."

Later that day the young man summarized the notes he had made:

The tenth secret of Abundant Wealth—the power of charity.

Abundance in anything is rarely achieved without help from other people or without helping other people.

By helping others, we help ourselves.

Try to give away ten percent of your income to help those in need. Whatever you give out will return to you multiplied.

Helping others impresses on your subconscious a feeling of abundance.

EPILOGUE

He closed the front door gently behind him so as not to wake his wife and children who were still asleep. It was dark, the day still yet to dawn, and wearing a tracksuit he made his way to the park. It was a ritual he had continued since his meeting with the mysterious old Chinese man.

As he walked, his mind drifted back to the morning they had met. So much had happened in the space of the five intervening years; it was still incredible, hardly believable to think of the massive changes that had occurred in his life.

Within a year of meeting him, the young man had managed to clear all of his debts and put aside ten percent of his earnings for savings and investment.

Six months later he had given up his job and set up his own small business publishing a newsletter for people who worked from home. It was a project he had thought of when he first considered setting up his own business because he found that there was very little available in terms of information, support or guidance for the growing number of people who were interested in working from home. He had needed to find out about such things as computer technology, taxation, legal matters, and the range of available services which were necessary for people who wanted to set up a business which they could run from their home.

The newsletter had been a resounding success, and eighteen months later he had completed his first book which was swiftly followed by six others over the following three years, of which five became international bestsellers.

In that time, he met and fell in love with a wonderful woman who he married and they now had two children on whom he doted. His family was, he would tell people, the real wealth in his life. Everything else was secondary; even without all of the money he had earned, without his house and without all of the other material possessions he owned, he would still consider himself a wealthy man. "After all," he would say, "what possible price could he put on the love, joy and happiness that his family gave him?"

People would occasionally ask him how he had managed to do so well. Those who had known him in the days when he struggled to cope were especially interested. Did he have a lucky break? Win the lottery? He told them about his meeting with a little old Chinese man and the secrets of Abundant Wealth. Few believed his story, but there were others who listened to what he had to say, and incorporated the secrets of Abundant Wealth into their own lives. Without exception, all of them had not only substantially increased their income but perhaps more importantly, so they told the young man, they had acquired something far more important than money, more precious than diamonds, and that was a different attitude to Life. No longer were they victims of circumstances, but masters of their own destinies. And, knowing that he had helped other people was, to the young man, the greatest feeling in the world. Any man is rich when he has experienced the joy of helping others.

Each morning as he walked through the park he hoped that he would see the old man again. He wanted to let the old man know what had happened in his life as a result of meeting him and learning the secrets of Abundant Wealth. He would have liked to thank him for everything he did for him. But this morning, like all of the others, there was no sign of the old man.

The sun was rising, revealing a clear blue sky when he returned home. The young man picked up the post and put the kettle on to make his wife a cup of tea. Suddenly the telephone rang, giving him a jolt. Seven in the morning was, by anybody's standards, an early time to call.

He picked up the receiver. A voice said, "Hello. You don't know me. My name is Arnold Banks. I'm sorry to call you so early but I have just met an old Chinese man who gave me your number and said that you would be able to explain something about . . . "

"The secrets of Abundant Wealth," interrupted the young man.

"Yes," answered the man on the phone, "the secrets of Abundant Wealth."

"Of course," said the young man, who could not conceal the joy from his voice. "It'll be my pleasure."

Adam J. Jackson is an internationally renowned therapist, author, and motivational speaker. He originally practiced law in England before retraining in natural health sciences. He currently lives in the United Kingdom and heads health clinics both there and in Toronto, Canada.